FUNDAMENTALS OF RIDING

FUNDAMENTALS OF
RIDING

Gregor de Romaszkan

TRANSLATED BY
M. A. STONERIDGE

•

WITH A FOREWORD BY
WILLIAM STEINKRAUS

1964

Doubleday & Company, Inc., Garden City, New York

This book was first published in Switzerland in 1942 by
Albert Müller Verlag, Rüschlikon-Zürich,
in the German language under the title Reiten Lernen.
The fourth edition was published in 1957.

LIBRARY OF CONGRESS CATALOG CARD NUMBER 64–19267
COPYRIGHT © 1964 BY GREGOR DE ROMASZKAN
FIRST EDITION IN THE UNITED STATES OF AMERICA

FOREWORD

It is axiomatic that the beginner in most activities must commence by learning the basic principles involved and practicing their application. The sport and art of riding are no exceptions, and the neophyte on horseback is urged from every quarter to "acquire a sound foundation."

What, then, goes wrong?

Why does it happen that so many novice riders abandon their equestrian pursuits at an early stage without ever coming within hailing distance of a sound foundation, or, sadder yet, persevere painfully for years while hardly coming any closer?

There are probably several different reasons. First of all, there is a type of beginner which stubbornly thinks of all horses in terms of "Old Dobbin," and refuses to identify riding as the kind of activity that merits or benefits from serious study. A closely related attitude, while conceding that riding *can* sustain serious thought and effort, wants no part of either. "I just want to ride for fun," say adherents of this view, "and thinking takes all the fun out of it."

For both groups, the "horseback ride" has a value that lies somewhere between an amusement park's "thrill ride" and vigorous Swedish massage. Regrettable though these misconceptions may be, little can be done to effect the equestrian salvation of their proponents, for they simply have no desire to be saved.

Of far more serious concern, however, are those enthusiastic, well-motivated beginners who really *want* to learn the right way and are willing to lavish on riding all the concentration and energy at their command. Sadly, they are often more sinned against than sinning, for frequently those who are designated to instruct them have little understanding themselves of the basic principles involved in riding, or, worse, a false understanding. This is not to say that the instructor cannot usually apply some of the basic principles in practice—through instinct or acquired habit—but he may not have a very clear understanding of *how* and *why* things happen the way they do.

"Heels down!" . . . "Elbows in!" . . . "Knees in" . . . This may all be good advice, but unless the beginner has some idea of *why* it's sound, it may be a long time before the shouting modulates.

"Pull your horse together!" . . . "Get *into* him!" . . . Yes, but how? And isn't it rather, "*Push* your horse together?" Some feel that the beginner must learn these things largely for himself, or perhaps only start to think about them "later on, when he's more advanced."

Though Gregor de Romaszkan addresses himself primarily to the novice who wants to start building a sound foundation *now*, I have no doubt that many experienced riders will also benefit from the extraordinarily clear and often original analysis of the physical and psychological relationships between horse and rider that is set forth on the pages that follow. Not only has he distilled for us the conclusions reached through a lifetime's study, but also provided, in his examination of alternate dogma, an object lesson in how to sift through contradictory theories.

"Life is short, and art is long," or, as Gregor de Romaszkan puts it, "There always remains an infinite amount to learn." Yes, there is plenty for the horseman to do without retracing his steps later on to shore up a flimsy or a false foundation. So for the beginner who would happily accede to the advice to "acquire a sound foundation," if only somebody would tell him precisely what it is or how it is acquired—let him turn the page.

CONTENTS

LIST OF PLATES

AUTHOR'S INTRODUCTION

While *Fundamentals of Riding* contains much material of interest even to an experienced rider, it is addressed primarily to beginners. Its aim is to teach them the principles of the art of equitation and the ways and means of becoming a good rider.

From the very first chapter the novice is immediately initiated into the "secrets"—or, rather, the basic principles—of horsemanship. Not only will he find an explanation of the correct forms of seat and the most effective use of the aids, but at the same time the underlying precepts of each lesson are pointed out in order to make them perfectly understandable. Merely learning how to ride does not transform a novice into a horseman. He must acquire along with his physical technique a knowledge of the fundamental laws by which this technique is governed. He should know not only *how* a horse will respond to his actions in the saddle, but also *why* the horse cannot or should not respond in any other way.

When an intelligent person possesses a thorough understanding of the task confronting him, he accomplishes it with more enthusiasm, and therefore better and more thoroughly, than when he is unaware of its significance and purpose. And so my hope is that through this book the thoughtful beginner will find genuine *enjoyment* in the sometimes arduous study of horsemanship, because he will have acquired a complete *understanding* of the principal riding problems.

In short, my aim is: *To guide him through understanding to pleasure and through pleasure to achievement.*

CHAPTER 1

SO YOU WANT
TO LEARN TO RIDE!

SO YOU WANT TO LEARN TO RIDE!

1. *Riding as a Sport*

Riding, aside from its practical applications, is widely practiced as a sport. But it holds a special place among all the other sports because its instrument is a living and breathing creature. Everything that can be achieved in riding depends on the mentality and feelings of this creature: the horse. And so the equestrian sport is unique, because it is in the first place an inexhaustible source of purely sporting pleasure and satisfaction, and, secondly, because it requires of the horseman certain qualities and talents that the other sports demand to a much lesser degree or not at all. The rider must possess not only such physical aptitudes as strength, dexterity, and endurance, but also such intellectual faculties as decisiveness, patience, presence of mind, and courage. He must also acquire a knowledge of physical, physiological, and psychological phenomena. Above all, he should possess a special *sensitivity* that is called *"equestrian tact."* When present, this undefinable quality permits an immediate understanding of all the physical and psychological circumstances encountered by the horse and rider, so that the rider can instinctively make the necessary adjustments in his attitude and actions. Equestrian tact is at the same time the foundation of *riding talent* and the measure of its potential development. Upon it depends the extent and quality of one's equestrian skill, whether it be merely Sunday-afternoon park hacking or the most advanced forms of the riding art.

Anybody can learn without too much difficulty to ride well enough to enjoy occasional jaunts on horseback, but few riders are equipped to become outstandingly successful even in one particular field of equitation. These achievements are reserved for the horsemen who not only possess the requisite inborn talent, but who, through constant effort and often even personal sacrifice, succeed in developing their natural gifts. Thus some modest beginners are able to obtain results of which they never dared to dream! You never can tell, when you first start learning to ride, just what degree of equestrian skill you may finally attain.

2.   *Riding as an Art*

Incontestably, riding is an *art*. Like all the other arts, it is based upon a certain sensitivity. This sensitivity, the horseman's riding talent, is a gift of nature. Either you have it or you don't. In the first case, it can be strengthened and developed; in the second, it can never be acquired. When it is lacking, you can, it is true, partially replace it by learning to exploit all of the technical resources that are available to the horseman. But you can never become a master, a true artist. You will always remain more or less an artisan.

How can you tell, before learning from experience, whether or not you possess this special talent?

No artist knows in advance whether or not he is talented, but somehow he *senses* it. His talent dominates his entire being, his thoughts, ideas, desires, and ambitions. It seeks expression and, unless prevented by external circumstances, leads him to success. Talent is a source of pleasure and also of the will power necessary to realize a definite goal. That is why this chapter is entitled: "So you *WANT* to learn to ride!"

No artist is born a master. Everything must be learned. It is the same with riding. We must therefore *learn* to ride. But how should we start?

Among the peoples living close to nature—the Indians and the Arabs, for example—riding was learned in a purely empirical manner. Primitive man succeeded by his own efforts alone in reaching a degree of skill and dexterity that was sometimes admirable—just as a puppy thrown into a pond starts swimming in order to avoid drowning. However, his art remains rather elementary—primitive, like himself. It will always lack the refinement that comes from a scientific knowledge of the laws of nature, combined with experience based on this knowledge. Culture and education are absent. In short, it is impossible to learn the true art of riding by a simple system of trial and error.

Of course, we can consult the mass of literature that civilized peoples have devoted to the art of equitation. But though we may study numerous volumes and try to draw from them the most important lessons, we will finally discover, when we attempt to profit from the knowledge we have thus acquired artificially, that we are incapable of putting it to practical use. It doesn't work. We can describe with ease and great detail the correct position in the saddle, and we may even succeed in utilizing our book learning when dealing with an immobile mount. But it is not at all the same when the mount begins to move! Our arms and legs no longer obey us, and the horse even less. We don't even realize what positions the different parts of our body are taking, nor the movements they are making. They are completely out of our control. All of our studies prove to be fruitless, and we end up by admitting that the art of riding is based upon a definite physical skill—a skill which we may understand very well in theory, but which can be acquired only through training and practice. That is why it is impossible to learn to ride from books, especially where the fundamental principles and the very first steps are concerned. Books serve merely to develop a more thorough understanding of the numerous riding problems. While they can be of great assistance to horsemen who wish to perfect their art, theory alone has never made a rider.

The art of riding is the practical application of static and dynamic mechanical laws and the principles of anatomy, physiology, and psychology, to oneself and to the horse. Therefore, it requires special knowledge and a great deal of training, leading in turn to greater knowledge. Theory and practice must be closely associated if we are to reach our goal. In other words, to become a good rider entails a veritable *education*—and education implies an educator. You cannot learn to ride really well without a *riding instructor.*

3. Learning to Ride

A good teacher, one who possesses a complete theoretical and practical mastery of all that concerns the equestrian art, plays an extremely important role in the rider's education. On the sureness of his perception depend the promptness and value of his judgment and advice in solving every individual problem. If he has a clear vision of the goal and of the paths that lead to it, he can easily guide his pupils by intelligently planned lessons, logical explanations, judicious comparisons, as well as by his own sound example.

But the results of riding lessons depend no less essentially upon the attitude of the pupil. The best teacher in the world cannot perform miracles, and he will obtain only mediocre results if he encounters a lack of receptivity. Every student should realize that success in riding is achieved only by personal, sustained effort, and that one must learn by oneself, with the help of the teacher. It is futile merely to place oneself passively in his hands, hoping that the teacher, by some supernatural means, will be able to inculcate all of the necessary knowledge.

Therefore, you must constantly be dominated by the idea expressed in the title of this chapter: *You must WANT to learn to ride!*

CHAPTER 2

LEARNING TO RIDE

LEARNING TO RIDE

1. *Mounting and Dismounting*

Having first been saddled and bridled,* the horse is led from
the stable. When using a snaffle bridle, the rider brings the snaffle
reins forward over the horse's head with his right hand, keeping
the reins separated by the index finger and holding them at about
a hand's width below the rings of the bit; the ends of the reins are
grasped by the left hand. When using a double bridle, the process
is identical because the curb reins should always remain on the
horse's neck. The rider is now standing on the horse's left side. He
hangs the snaffle reins over the left arm and prepares to mount
in the saddle. But first of all he must check the saddle and bridle
to make sure that the snaffle, the curb, and the curb chain are properly placed, that the throat latch is not too tight, and that the girth
is tight enough. Now he pulls down the stirrup irons and adjusts
the leathers to their approximate length, which is just about the
same as his outstretched arm. The ends of the leathers should not
be pushed inside and through the buckle, but turned under the
stirrup leathers themselves, from front to back, in order to permit

* The only suitable bridle for a novice rider or a young horse is the snaffle. Advanced riders and trained horses may use a double bridle, but only for specialized
dressage.

the rider to adjust the length conveniently when he is in the saddle (Fig. 1).

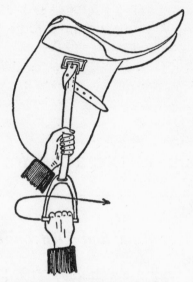

FIG. 1. *How to pull the end of the stirrup leather under the leather itself and how to place the stirrup irons correctly.*

It is sometimes helpful, particularly when the stirrup leathers are new, to twist the irons several times toward the rear; when they are released, they will tend to hang perpendicularly rather than parallel to the horse's body, thus enabling them to be more easily recovered by the rider's foot.

During all of these preparations, the reins have been looped over the left arm. Now they are passed over the horse's head and laid on its neck, and the rider is ready to mount.

The *mounting* procedure, and in fact everything concerning the utilization of horses, used to be precisely regulated in the cavalry. Most civilian riding instructors advocate the traditional army method of mounting, which is as follows:

The rider, who is on the left side of the horse with his right hand holding the reins on the horse's neck, standing at the horse's head and looking in the direction of the head, makes a quarter turn and one step to the right, so that he is now facing the horse's left shoulder. The right hand then slides to the end of the reins, while the left hand grasps the reins on the horse's neck along with a portion of the horse's mane. The reins should be very slightly taut and separated by the fingers. If the rider carries a riding crop, he holds it too in the left hand, along the horse's shoulder and pointing toward the ground. Then the ends of the reins are thrown over to the right side of the neck. The rider makes almost a quarter turn to the right, grasps the lower part of the stirrup leather with his right hand and slips his left foot into the stirrup, taking care to avoid jabbing the horse with his toe. He places the right hand on the cantle, springs from the right foot and raises himself above the saddle. The right hand then moves to the pommel, the right leg swings over the croup, after which the rider lets himself slide smoothly into the saddle. He then grasps the reins with both hands in the normal fashion and slips the right foot into the right stirrup without looking down.

The most important points in this procedure are the following:

1. Before placing the left foot in the stirrup, the rider, facing the horse's left shoulder, makes almost a quarter turn to the right, which places him in the direction of its right hip. The moment when he places his foot in the stirrup and is only touching the ground with the other is a rather critical one for him, because the slightest forward or backward movement of the horse can throw him off his balance. The position that has just been described permits him to regain any possible loss of equilibrium by simply hopping on the right foot either forward or backward. Likewise, as soon as the rider has taken hold of the cantle with his right hand, he can no longer be thrown down if the horse should move forward; on the contrary, the movement would more or less throw him into the saddle. Both of these things would be impossible if he were facing the saddle.

2. As soon as the rider has placed his left foot in the stirrup, the only way he can avoid touching the horse's body with the tip of his toe—especially if the horse is big—is by turning the tip of his toe toward the rear and by pressing his knee a little to the side against the saddle skirt. When he rises from the ground and lets himself down into the saddle, the knee turns first toward the horse and then toward the front, while the tip of the toe, pointing

to the rear, describes an arc underneath the horse's body, finally turning to the front.

3. In pulling himself up, the rider should maintain his balance by leaning sufficiently forward and by supporting himself on his hands, rather than by placing all of his weight on the stirrup. The upper part of the body will lean even farther forward at the moment when the rider, supported by his right hand on the pommel, swings his leg above the croup (which he should not touch) in a large circular movement. By seeking support from his right hand and by closing the knees and thighs, it is possible for him to slide gently into the saddle instead of falling into it with a thud.

4. If, however, the horse is jabbed either in the belly by the tip of the toe or in the croup by the right foot, or if it is jolted by the rider's weight suddenly descending on its back, you should not expect the animal to remain calm and still. These riding faults often cause a horse—especially nervous ones—to develop bad habits and vices that are difficult to cure.

In order *to dismount*, the rider first takes the reins and a portion of mane in his left hand, and releases the right stirrup. Then, resting his right hand on the pommel, he lifts himself above the saddle, passes his right leg over the croup, and shifts his right hand from the pommel to the cantle, so that he finds himself placed sideways on the horse. He can continue to dismount in two different ways: he can either keep the left foot in the stirrup until the right foot has touched the ground, or—which is better—he can slip out of the left stirrup and jump or slide to the ground.

To vault into the saddle, the rider passes the reins, which have been lying on the horse's neck, over his left arm. He faces the saddle, grasps the pommel with his left hand and the cantle with his right hand; then he springs off both feet to place himself laterally suspended over the saddle. Now, supporting himself on the pommel with both hands, he swings the right leg over the croup and lets himself slide down into the saddle. He takes the reins in the normal manner and slips his feet into the stirrups.

This method of mounting is not only an excellent physical exercise, but also of great practical value. Every rider should be able to mount without the aid of stirrups.

To jump down from the saddle, the rider slips both feet out of the stirrups, places his left hand to the left and his right hand to the right of the pommel, and leans his body somewhat backward while stretching his legs forward. He then throws his outstretched legs vigorously backward, letting the heels touch as he leans the upper part of his body toward the horse's neck and supports himself on his arms; he swings his legs over the croup and jumps to the ground on the left side of the horse.

Every rider should be able to dismount in this way.

Mounting with assistance is a common practice when a groom leads out the horse, and also when dealing with very young horses. The rider uses his left hand in the normal fashion, but he does not put his foot in the stirrup and the right hand grasps the pommel instead of the cantle. Then he bends his left knee and is "given a leg up" by the groom, who places a hand under the bent left leg. This way of mounting, especially when the stirrups are short, is much more convenient, not only for the horseman, but also for the horse. Furthermore, there is no risk of the saddle's being turned.

All of these exercises, as well as the first lessons concerning the correct seat and how to hold the reins, can be practiced very profitably on a wooden horse.

2. *The Seat*

The rider's seat is correct when he does not disturb the horse's balance, and thereby offers it the possibility of carrying him as effortlessly as possible and of producing free, secure, and ample movements—in other words, the highest possible degree of efficiency.

But this can be achieved only if the rider is seated vertically above the horse's center of gravity, and consequently in accordance with its weight vector.* In this way, the weight of the rider is distributed *equally* on the forehand and the hindquarters (as well as on both sides of the horse) and the horse's legs are thus burdened in the *same natural ratio* as when they are sharing the weight of its own mass. We then say: *The rider is sitting in equilibrium.*

The rider is not sitting in equilibrium when his own mass and that of the horse act on two different weight vectors, that is, when the rider's weight vector deviates from that of the horse either to the front, to the rear, or to one side or the other. In these instances, the rider's weight overburdens the horse's front, hind, or lateral pairs of legs, disturbing the animal's balance, diminishing its weight-bearing capacity, and making its movements heavy, insecure, and lacking in impulsion.

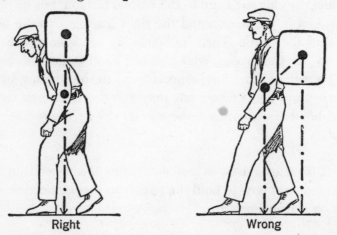

Right   Wrong

FIG. 2. *The easiest way to carry a burden is to place it in such a way that its center of gravity is above our own.*

It is simple to prove for yourself that the easiest and most convenient way of carrying a burden is to place it so that its center of gravity is above your own, with both of them on the same vertical plane (Fig. 2). There is no reason why it should not be exactly the same when the horse is the carrier and the rider is the burden.

* The imaginary line drawn perpendicularly from the center of gravity to the ground, indicating the action of the force of gravity, is called the "weight vector."

The location of *the horse's center of gravity* depends upon its individual conformation as well as on the particular momentary position of its head, neck, back, and legs, that is to say, on its *posture*. When a horse is at liberty and is holding itself normally, its center of gravity is approximately at the point where a vertical line traced immediately behind the withers meets a horizontal line traced from the shoulder joint to the buttock (Fig. 3).

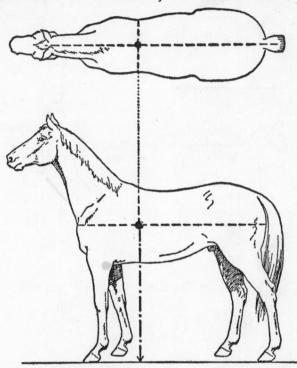

FIG. 3. *The location of the horse's center of gravity.*

This point is continually displaced by every change in the horse's posture. A shortening of the neck (cervical lever), produced by raising and flexing it, shifts the center of gravity toward the rear; a horizontal extension of the neck (lengthening) moves it forward (Fig. 4), and a lateral flexion of the neck displaces it sideways in the direction of the flexion (Fig. 5).

In a normal seat on a horse that is in a natural, relaxed posture, the rider is not in equilibrium with his mount. In order to achieve this state, he must induce the horse to take a shorter posture at

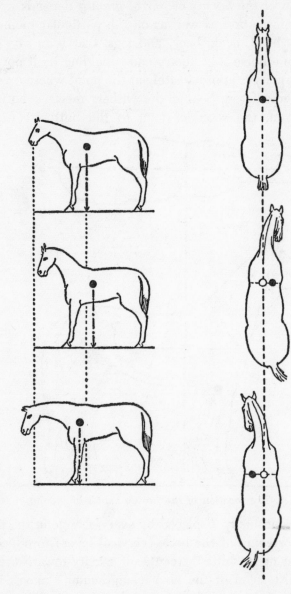

FIG. 4. *The horse's posture can change the location of its center of gravity: a shortening of the neck shifts the center of gravity to the rear; a lengthening moves it forward.*

FIG. 5. *A lateral flexion of the neck displaces the center of gravity sideways in the direction of the flexion.*

the shorter gaits, thereby shifting its center of gravity toward the rear and placing it underneath the rider's seat. During fast movements which require the horse to extend itself, the rider should adapt himself to the new conditions by displacing his body weight so as to bring it in line with the more forward center of gravity, that is to say, he must take a more or less forward seat (Fig. 6). The first condition occurs during schooling in the riding

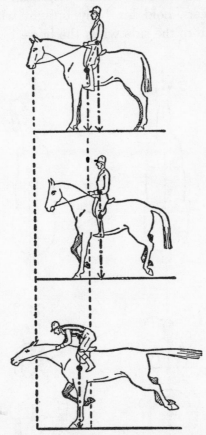

FIG. 6. *In order to sit in equilibrium with his mount, the rider must induce the horse to take a shorter posture or he must adapt his seat to the extended position of the horse.*

ring and in dressage riding, the rider balancing his horse at the shorter gaits; the second case is that of the rider who "accompanies" the horse's movements during jumping or racing.

Consequently, we can distinguish between: 1. The full seat,

customary at all the gaits at which the horse's body must be shortened: the halt, walk, trot, and collected canter; 2. The half seat
(forward seat), which permits the rider to sit in equilibrium at all
extended paces, such as the gallop and when jumping; and 3. The
racing seat, which is suitable only for the extremely extended
movements of horses on the race track.

In order to maintain the lateral equilibrium as well, the rider
should, in all seats, hold his body upright when the horse is
straight, and lean to the side when the horse bends its body laterally (Fig. 7).

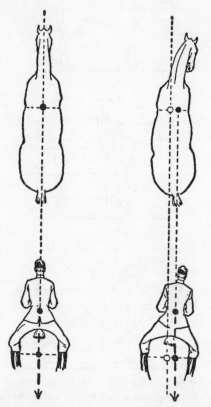

FIG. 7. *In order to maintain the lateral equilibrium, the rider should hold
his body upright when the horse is straight and lean to the side when the
horse bends its body laterally.*

The rider can shift his weight correctly only when his seat is
unconstrained, supple, and secure. In order to achieve this, he
must have previously assured *his own balance* on the horse's back

with the least possible muscular effort, which means that he must be *in balance*. In a correct seat, all of the muscles are relaxed and constantly ready to obey, with suppleness, the rider's commands. It is very easy to assume this seat on a stationary horse, but it is quite another matter when the animal's movements become rapid or violent, bringing into play a set of muscles which is ordinarily seldom used and therefore inadequately developed in the novice rider. And so it is not sufficient to know what is the correct seat to take; one must also acquire, through training, the ability to maintain it.

The seat is not an end in itself, but the means of attaining a definite goal. *It should result from a natural and appropriate response of the rider to the horse.* In no case should he merely adopt a particular style that has been chosen arbitrarily. When a school, for example, attempts to obtain a certain uniformity of style, it should be achieved not by artificial drilling, but by developing among the riders *a unity of conception as to their equestrian principles and goals.* This is the only way to acquire an elastic, supple, secure seat, which permits the rider to feel and to control his horse at every instant with precision, and above all *to sit in equilibrium*, that is, in their *common* equilibrium.

The rider's posture should therefore be natural and appropriate and not merely an imitation of a so-called model seat. Stiffness in the seat almost always originates in the desire to copy indiscriminately some pose or other, frequently recommended by the riding instructor himself as being the only correct and attractive one, but in no way corresponding to the personal qualities of the rider. Once the habit has been formed, it is extremely difficult to break, and consequently to acquire a seat that is *truly correct* for the individual rider and not merely the imitation of another one considered to be aesthetic.

Once we have acknowledged the essential principle of the seat, which is to remain in equilibrium, the primary goal of equestrian training is then to give the rider such a control over his *own* balance that he loses all apprehension of falling, which is usually his strongest fear. That is why it is necessary, at the beginning, to reduce to the strictest minimum the control he is required to exercise over the horse, and even to eliminate it entirely (by group training in a single file, or by training on a longeing rein) in order to teach the rider to preserve his equilibrium, in other words, to remain in balance. It is only when he is able to remain in the saddle, not by clinging with his hands and legs, but as a simple function of balance, that he can progress to the following stage, which is to learn the principles of influencing the horse by utilizing the resultant freedom of his limbs.

The rider's posture is determined by five essential points, which are the head, the hands, the seat, the knees, and the heels. If all of these parts of the body work together in a supple, harmonious, and efficient manner, the seat is correct and need not be modified (Fig. 8).

FIG. 8. *The rider's posture is determined by five essential points, which are the head, the hands, the seat, the knees and the heels.*

The *full seat* offers the greatest security in the saddle and the best capability for influencing the horse. It is therefore of prime importance in equitation. The rider supports the upper part of his body, which is held erect, on his seat bones in the deepest part of the saddle. The small of the back can thus be more or less contracted or stretched according to the particular circumstances. But it should never be hollowed, for this is likely to stiffen the entire position and render impossible the supple contact with the horse's back that is so important in the full seat. The rider's gaze should be directed in the distance over the horse's head. His shoulders and arms are relaxed, the forearms lightly touching the body. The hands, whose joints remain supple, are closed without being clenched. The thighs slant forward and the knees are lightly pressed against the saddle. The lower part of the leg should slope backward along the rear edge of the girth and remain in light contact with the horse's flank. The balls of the feet rest supplely in the stirrups, while the heels are pressed toward the ground and slightly turned toward the horse's body.

The important point in the full seat is for the two seat bones (the two lowest bones of the pelvis) to exert an absolutely even pressure in the middle of the saddle (in actual practice, as close as possible to the pommel), so that the heels are contained in the same transversal plane as the upper part of the body. If the rider is seated farther back, it is called an "armchair seat"; if the seat bones rest insufficiently in the saddle, it is a "straddled" or "crotch" seat (Fig. 9); if the seat bones are displaced laterally or if the hips

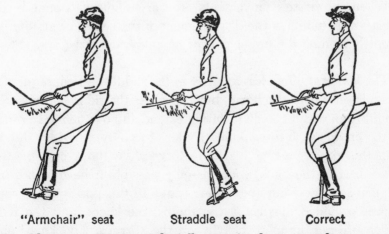

"Armchair" seat   Straddle seat   Correct

FIG. 9. *The important point of the full seat is for the two seat bones to exert an even pressure in the middle of the saddle.*

are turned in, it is an "oblique seat." In all of these positions, the upper part of the body no longer remains vertical, and consequently the posture is no longer correct or effective (Fig. 10).

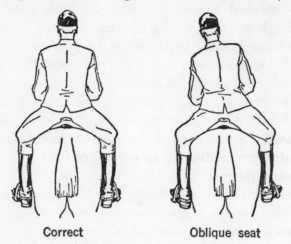

Correct   Oblique seat

FIG. 10. *If the seat bones are displaced laterally or the hips are turned in, the seat becomes oblique.*

The full seat is employed when the horse is standing still or moving on the flat at a walk, a (collected) trot, or a (collected) canter, as well as during all the other movements that necessitate a shortening of its body, such as certain exercises which are practiced in the riding ring or which form a part of high-school dressage (Fig. 11).

When the horse's movements are very slightly extended, the rider is able to follow the displacement of the center of gravity by supplely leaning the upper part of his body forward (Fig. 11).

The *half seat* offers less security in the saddle and consequently less influence over the horse, but it enables the rider to remain in equilibrium with his mount during extended movements. In order to stay in line with the animal's center of gravity, the rider should lean the upper part of his body forward, without curving the lower part of the back, which is only possible if he modifies his original seat by rising above the saddle. In this position, the support is provided mostly by the thighs, the knees, and the feet, which press a bit more heavily on the stirrups. The knees and heels should be held as low as possible.

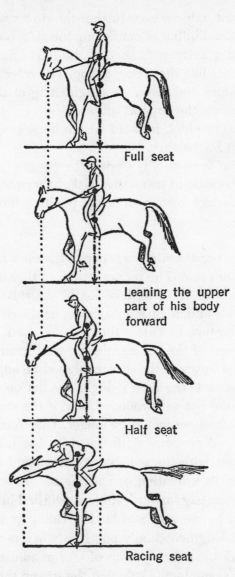

Full seat

Leaning the upper
part of his body
forward

Half seat

Racing seat

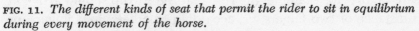

FIG. 11. *The different kinds of seat that permit the rider to sit in equilibrium during every movement of the horse.*

This seat is used for the extended canter or gallop and for jumping, in particular for show jumping and hacking over rough terrain. In the course of the rider's training, the half seat should be learned by using as a foundation the principles that govern the full seat (Fig. 11).

The *racing seat* reduces even further the rider's security in the saddle and the possibilities of employing the aids, but it aligns the rider's center of gravity with that of the horse during very extended movements like the racing gallop. The rider abandons the grip with his thighs and relies on a tightening of the knees and calves as well as on the support afforded by very short stirrups, while the hands, reaching forward on the horse's neck, also help him to maintain his balance.

The racing seat is used only during the maximum extension of the horse and, because of its relatively slight security, over rather short distances, which means, in actual practice, only at the race track (Fig. 11).

The *adjustment of the stirrups* is one of the most important elements of the rider's seat. The proper length of the stirrup leathers depends, not only on the length of leg of the rider, but also on their conformation and, to no less a degree, on the conformation of the horse and the type of saddle that is being used. If the rider's thighs are rounded, if the horse's ribs are well sprung, and if the saddle flaps slope forward, the stirrups should be adjusted higher. On the other hand, if the rider's thighs are flat on the inside, if the horse's ribs are not very rounded, and if the saddle flaps are cut straight, the leathers should be longer. Therefore, the stirrups cannot be adjusted properly until the rider has taken a correct seat in the saddle, with the seat bones, knees, and heels in their proper positions. In a hunting or hacking saddle with flaps that are cut only moderately forward, stirrups adjusted in this way will be well adapted to every normal kind of riding and will need to be shortened or lengthened only one hole when performing special exercises. All the other systems of stirrup adjustment are unsatisfactory; for example, the rule that the stirrup should arrive at a distance of two fingers, or, according to others, four fingers, or even an entire hand above the foot when the leg is hanging free. These methods can only furnish approximate results and are valid only for a specific type of saddle.

The instructor should carefully supervise the adjustment of his pupils' stirrups. He can influence the training by varying the length up or down, depending on the defects he may have noted in the rider's seat.

Every horseman should be able to adjust his stirrup leathers from the saddle unaided. He should accomplish this with one hand, while his foot remains in the stirrup, helping to shorten or lengthen the leather (Fig. 12).

FIG. 12. *The rider should be able to adjust his stirrup leathers from the saddle.*

3. *The Aids*

As soon as his seat is sufficiently secure and the rider has thus acquired a certain freedom of action, he can begin to learn how to control and influence the horse.

The means at his disposal for communicating with the horse and for inducing it to submit to his will are called *"the aids."* They are: 1. the legs; 2. the hands (through the intermediary of the reins and bit); and 3. the weight of his body.

The *leg aids* are driving (impelling) actions and are produced by a pressure of the lower part of the limb, which is placed with a certain deviation from the vertical along the girth, more precisely, at its rear edge. The knees (held flat), and the heels (slightly turned toward the horse's flanks—a little like their position when walking) should be as low as possible. If the knees are not against the saddle, the rider's position is weakened and the

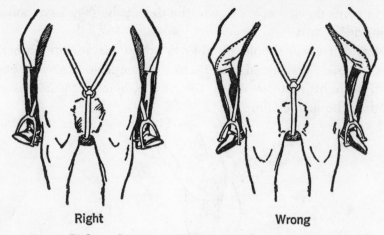

Right   Wrong

FIG. 13. *Right and wrong position of the knees, legs, and heels.*

legs are unable to act correctly (Fig. 13). The angle formed by
the upper and lower parts of the leg depends upon the length of
the stirrup leathers, which in turn depends upon the type of seat
as well as the length of the rider's legs and the degree of curvature
of the horse's ribs. The rider presses the balls of his feet on the
stirrup in a light and supple manner—somewhat stronger in the
half seat. (In no case should the horse be girdled by the legs, and
the assertion that most horsemen end up with bowlegs is completely unfounded!)

In the racing seat, the rider's foot is pushed "home" in the stirrup, as far as the heel, and the stirrups, which more or less bear
the weight of his body, are adjusted very short.

The rider's leg actions may be: 1. passive; or 2. active. Needless
to add, when we say passive, we mean it in a relative sense, for it
is not an absolute passivity, which has no place in equitation. If it
can be said that the active (driving) aids enable the rider to "talk"
to the horse, we can consider the passive (sensitive) aids as enabling him to "listen" to the horse.

In the first (passive) case, the legs remain in constant contact
with the horse's flanks and make no demands.

In the second (active) case, they act by squeezing or tapping
on the horse's flanks and can: 1. urge the horse forward; 2. urge
the horse to the side; or 3. restrain evasions.

The driving action, to obtain a forward movement, is applied on the girth, at its rear edge. The lateral action, to obtain a sideways movement, and the restraining action, to prevent an evasion of one of the hind legs, are both applied a hand's width behind the girth.

As a general rule, all of them should be executed by means of a supple and continuous pressure which is gradually increased until the desired effect has been obtained. The tapping or kicking action is permissible only in certain circumstances, most often in cases of disobedience, and it is therefore punitive in character.

The rider's legs act indirectly on the corresponding hind legs of the horse. In other words, an action of the rider's right leg influences the horse's right hind leg—"indirectly" because it does not of course actually come in contact with the hind leg.

The *rein aids* are restraining actions that function on the bit through the intermediary of the hands and reins. The rider's arms, hanging free, bend at the elbows and normally form a more or less open angle. The forearms are directed forward in an absolutely straight line with the reins. The wrists, always supple, form, along with the backs of the hands, a prolongation of the straight line of the forearms and may be sometimes slightly turned toward the inside, but never outward. The hands, which should be closed but not clenched, hold the reins. They should assume a natural position, that is, the thumbs should not be turned down, nor should they be held too straight upright, but slightly inclined so that, if the hands were holding sticks, these would cross in front of the rider's chest. Any lack of naturalness in the hand position produces stiffness in the wrists and prevents manipulating the reins in an adroit and supple manner. The distance between the hands as well as the height at which they are held depends upon the horse's head carriage and the size of its neck, and also on the width of the rider's chest and the type of rein action. The correct distance from the body is one which allows the hands the same amount of space in which to move both forward and backward.

The manner in which the reins are held depends upon the type of bridle used. They may be held with two hands (divided reins) or only one. With a snaffle, they are held in two hands, passing between the fourth and fifth fingers (Fig. 14). With a double

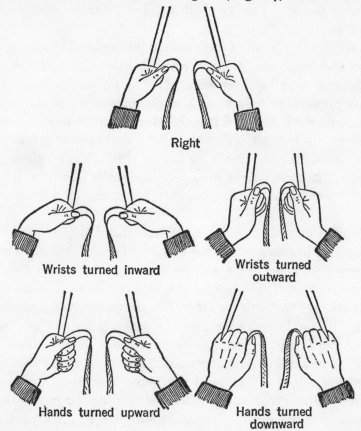

Right

Wrists turned inward   Wrists turned outward

Hands turned upward   Hands turned downward

FIG. 14. *Right and wrong ways of holding the reins when using a snaffle bridle.*

bridle, when they are held in both hands, the snaffle reins are separated from the curb reins by the fifth finger, with the snaffle reins passing underneath the little finger. When the double reins are held in only one hand, the left snaffle and curb are held in just the same way, but the right curb passes between the fourth and third fingers of the left hand, and the right snaffle between the third and second fingers. In what is termed the "dressage method" the left snaffle and the two curb reins remain in the left hand, while the right snaffle is held between the fourth and fifth fingers of the right hand (Fig. 15).

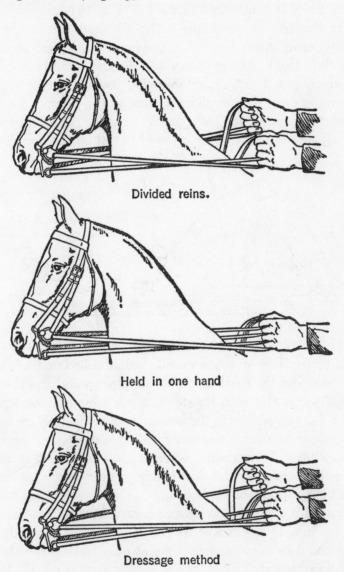

Divided reins.

Held in one hand

Dressage method

FIG. 15. *How to hold the reins when using a double bridle.*

In all methods, the reins run upward across the palm and emerge above the index finger, where they are retained by the thumb, and then hang down along the right side of the horse's neck (or, in certain systems, on the left side). When they are held in both hands, the ends of the reins should fall to the inside of the taut section that is attached to the bit (Fig. 15).

When the reins are held only in the left hand, the best method is to rest the right hand on the left one, or else to place it, closed, on the right thigh. In any case, the right arm should never hang free, which usually results in throwing back the right shoulder and thereby creating a crooked posture in the rider.

The hands holding the reins should never be turned downward (Fig. 16), nor should they be allowed to rest on the horse's neck,

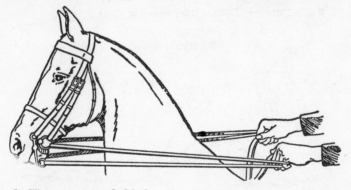

FIG. 16. *Wrong way to hold the reins (with hands turned downward).*

since their freedom of action would be diminished and, above all, they would lose their indispensable suppleness and therefore the possibility of acting with finesse, with the eventual consequence of dulling the sensitivity of the horse's mouth. The only exceptions to this rule occur during the racing gallop and when riding across rough country, for example, when negotiating steep slopes—in other words, whenever the rider is unable to maintain his balance without the support of his hands.

Riding with a curb always requires greater skill because of the powerful lever-like action of its cheekpieces, and it should only be attempted by students who have already learned to ride with a snaffle. Even then, the curb chain should be attached very loosely during the early lessons.

The hands can act: 1. passively; or 2. actively.

The passive action of the hands makes no demands on the horse. They merely adapt themselves to the horse's mouth, with which they maintain a very light and constant contact, determined by the degree of support the horse seeks from the bit. This contact should be permanently assured by the rider's driving actions, which, according to the state of balance, should be as light as possible during short paces, but correspondingly stronger during extended paces. It is when the horse is moving at a racing gallop that it requires the greatest support from the reins as a supplementary prop because of the extreme forward displacement of the center of gravity. This support from the reins is the horse's "fifth foot."

Riding with passive hands requires a great deal of tact and poses so difficult a problem to the rider that many of them, even among the most expert, do not succeed in solving it completely.

The effect of the active hands is: 1. to restrain; and 2. to support.

In the first case, the hands exert a progressive but elastic pulling until the desired reaction has been obtained. A restraining action by both reins produces a reduction of the rhythm, a transition from an extended pace to a shorter one (half halt), a halt (parade), and a rein-back (stepping backward). When one hand exerts a restraining action and the other remains passive, the effect obtained is lateral flexion and a change of direction.

When affording support, the hands are firm and immobile. This rein effect more or less transforms the bit into a sort of bolt that limits the horse's extension as desired.

If a horse pulls on the reins, the rider should not attempt to restrain it by pulling too. The horse is stronger than man and will always emerge victorious from such a struggle, especially if it is of long duration. Only by employing his strength in a rational manner can the rider succeed in making his own will triumph. Therefore, he should restrain the horse by a short, energetic rein action (which is not at all the same thing as a cruel yank on the bit), and as soon as the desired reduction of pace has been obtained, he should return to a normal, supple contact. This maneuver should be repeated until the horse has understood that the only way it can escape from the disagreeable action of the reins is to remain in the pace the rider desires.

As a general rule, the reins should always act in a straight line from front to rear. When changing the direction, the outside hand, which maintains a passive contact with the horse's mouth, should move forward exactly the same distance that the inside hand is drawn back, rather like the hand position of a bicyclist when he is making a turn (Fig. 17) with his hands on the handlebars.

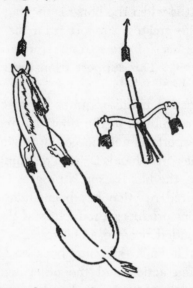

FIG. 17. *When changing direction, the outside hand should move forward exactly the same distance that the inside hand is drawn back.*

Never should a forward movement be obtained by yielding with the reins. It should result only from the driving action of the legs, while the hands passively follow the head and neck as they are stretched forward according to the movement. Many horsemen commit the serious error of riding their horses too much with their hands and not enough with their legs.

The *weight aids* can also be either 1. passive; or 2. active.

In the first case, the rider shifts his weight, thereby modifying his seat, in order to bring it in line with the horse's center of gravity and consequently to adapt himself to the horse's equilibrium. In doing so, he demands nothing of the horse. His only idea is to conform to the horse's movement in a passive and supple manner in order to allow his mount the greatest possible freedom of action.

In the second case, the rider uses his body weight actively in order to exert a calculated influence on the horse's posture and consequently on the position of its center of gravity. He obliges the animal to modify its equilibrium and, as a result, its movements.

If necessary, the rider can even employ his body weight so vigorously that its effect on the horse's back becomes a painful punishment.

By shifting his weight forward, the rider—in accordance with the laws of mechanics—provokes an extension of the horse and thus a lengthening of movement. By shifting it to the rear, he induces the horse to shorten its posture and movement. A shift of weight to the right or left causes a corresponding displacement of the horse's center of gravity and thereby influences its inflexion (in other words, the lateral bending of its body) and its direction.

It is the influence of the rider's weight, used in conjunction with the other aids, that produces a decisive effect on the horse's performance and enables the rider to exercise control over the animal in every situation and at every point.

The *spurs* serve to reinforce the leg aids and are employed when the horse obeys only partially or not at all. In such cases, the pressure of the leg is gradually increased until the spur comes in contact with the horse's flank and, if necessary, the contact becomes a prick.

When this action is ineffective or if the horse continues to resist, the spur may be used as a punishment. The rider gives a sharp prick, which should always be executed with the knees closed, behind the girth. The punishment is repeated until the horse yields. However, when employing this corrective measure, it is important to make sure that it is not disproportionate to the fault, which is a frequent occurrence with short-tempered riders. Furthermore, it should be applied only to willfully disobedient horses, and not to animals who simply do not understand the rider's demands immediately or who, for physical reasons, are incapable of responding to them. Punishment, like reward, should instantaneously follow the motivating incident; otherwise, the horse could easily become confused as to its significance, in which case it would do more harm than good.

With horses that are very sensitive or ticklish, dull spurs should be used. With some of them, it is even advisable to ride without spurs.

Beginners should never wear spurs until they have mastered the correct action of the leg aids. But even then, they must be taught beforehand how the spurs should be used.

The best kind is spurs *à la chevalière* (fastened by buckles). They should be attached so that they remain in place above the heels, for otherwise it is impossible to employ them correctly.

The *riding crop* may be made of various materials and in different forms. However, it can fulfill its function only if it is flexible without being flabby. When struck, it should not touch the horse's body with its entire length. One of the best kinds, and not the costliest, is made of rattan, and should be twenty-eight to thirty inches long, a finger's breadth in thickness, and smooth-surfaced. Whalebone and fiber glass are also excellent but considerably more expensive. Sticks made entirely of rawhide, rubber, or steel should be avoided at all cost.

The crop is useful when riding young horses who have not yet learned to understand the leg aids; for correcting spoiled animals who respond badly to these aids; and finally, for obliging a horse to jump a very wide obstacle or to produce an extreme degree of extension at the race track. But it is unnecessary with well-trained horses.

Green horses may acquire a better understanding of the leg aids if they are given light taps of the crop behind the active leg, or in certain circumstances (such as disobedience) on the shoulder. A tap applied behind the rider's leg, at the moment when the muscles begin to relax, obtains a more rapid and greater extension of these muscles and consequently a longer stride. In order to be prepared for any eventuality, the rider should be able to use the crop with either hand. But it is not a simple instrument to utilize, and a stick in inexpert hands can do more harm than good.

SCHOOL RIDING   1. The Walk.

SCHOOL RIDING   2. The Trot.

SCHOOL RIDING   3. The Canter.

SCHOOL RIDING   4. Turn on the hindquarters to the right.

4. Co-ordination of the Aids

Considered separately, the aids of the legs, reins, and weight provide the rider with only a very limited means of control. But when they are *combined effectively,* the results are decisive. Only a co-ordination of all the aids permits the rider to influence the horse successfully *as a whole,* and not merely certain individual parts of its body. The effect of the aids should penetrate with suppleness the horse's entire body and act on every part of it. When a horse allows itself to be ridden in this fashion, without any show of resistance, it is said to be *"responsive."*

Fundamentally, the rider operates the combined actions of the aids by using his entire spine and particularly the small of the back, which plays the role of an elastic organ of liaison. The position of the small of the back—whether it is straight or inclined, contracted or relaxed—determines to a considerable degree the *type and strength* and consequently the *efficacy and success* of all the rider's actions on the horse.

In order to employ the different aids correctly, and even more in order to combine them, the rider must first of all possess great sensitivity.

This sensitivity, which is called *"equestrian tact,"* is the rider's ability to sense all of the factors involved in his maintenance of control over the horse and in its possibilities of performance.

First of all, the rider must possess an accurate awareness of his seat, that is, of the position of his body and legs and therefore of *his own balance.* Furthermore, he must also feel all of the horse's movements, its gaits, rhythm, and pace, even its abilities and its intentions. Only under these conditions can he successfully co-ordinate the actions of the aids, complement one aid with another, and adapt them to the horse's temperament, sensitivity, and degree of training.

A talented rider will eventually acquire a feeling for the horse's posture, and a sense of how its balance can be altered by the extension, shortening, and flexion of its body. Only thus is it possible for the rider to maintain perfect equilibrium, which is a prerequisite to utilizing the horse's maximum capabilities. This sensitivity is what makes riding an art. Only riders who are especially gifted in this respect will be able to realize exceptional achievements.

Equestrian tact, as we have seen, is a talent that must be inborn, but it can be awakened, developed, and improved by training, and this is one of the principal tasks of the riding instructor. Nevertheless, in actual practice, the best instructor is the horse itself. It is on a well-schooled mount that the beginner acquires most quickly the right feeling for his seat and his actions, for the movements of the horse, and finally for their *common equilibrium*, which is the fundamental problem of the entire art of riding. Later on, the student masters the other rules and perfects his knowledge by riding and training green horses.

A horse is *"on the aids"* when it accepts their contact, understands their actions, and willingly submits to them. In order to obtain this result, the rider should employ all of them, and especially the driving aids.

The *leg aids,* to which the horse should respond perfectly, play a particularly important role. It is only during forward movement, with the impulsion that constitutes the principal element of equitation, that the horse can be placed on the aids correctly. Without impulsion, and without a constant willingness on the part of the horse to extend itself at any moment the rider desires, such a result is impossible.

The *rein aids,* in order to function correctly and effectively, must act on the most sensitive part of the horse's mouth, which is the bars. There should thus be created a permanent and supple contact between the rider's hands and the horse's mouth, which is called "support." If it is established correctly, the horse is said to be *"in hand"* or *"on the bit."* But a proper contact can be realized only if the horse's head and neck are held in a certain position in relation to the reins. Obtaining this position should be one of the rider's principal preoccupations (Fig. 18).

Can a horse resist the action of the reins? And, if so, to what extent? The answer to these questions depends partly on the

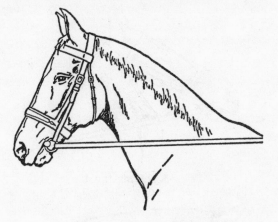

FIG. 18. *The horse is "in hand."*

horse's physical conformation and character, and partly on the rider's tact and skill in utilizing the aids. In order to evade the disagreeable action of the bit on the bars, the horse tries, by raising or lowering its head and neck, to shift this action onto the corners of the lips, which are more elastic and much less sensitive, or to annul the action by holding its head vertically, or even by drawing its mouth back still further. When the horse raises its head too high, it is said to be *"over the bit"* or *"above the hands"*; when it lowers the head excessively, it is *"under the bit"*; and when it pulls back the mouth, it places itself *"behind the bit"* (Fig. 19).

When a horse gets "over the bit," it usually decreases the pace; when "under the bit," it often extends the pace. In both cases, the rider should try above all to maintain an even pace and never allow the horse to slow down. By offering support with the reins, sometimes for a moment with only one rein, the rider obliges the horse to seek for itself a more comfortable position of the head and neck. In the meantime, at the slightest attempt made by the horse to lower the head and neck in the first case, or to raise them in the second, the rider should immediately change over to a passive action of the hands in order to reassure the animal and to encourage it to maintain the preferred position.

The rider must normally perform this task, which consists essentially of effectively and judiciously exerting an agreeable or disagreeable action on the horse's mouth, without resorting to

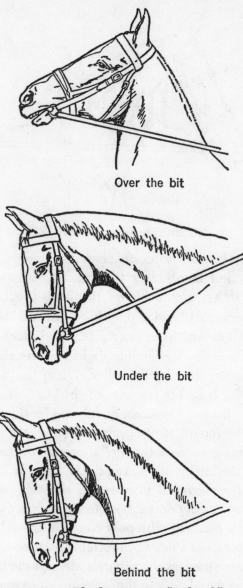

Over the bit

Under the bit

Behind the bit

FIG. 19. *The horse is not "in hand."*

auxiliary means. (At the very most, when it seems to be indispensable, he might utilize an ordinary martingale; but only temporarily, until the desired result has been obtained.) The simplest and most successful method is to force the horse to turn in a circle (volte), which, firstly, makes it easier to maintain an even pace and, secondly, obliges the inward-flexed horse to accept the action of the inside rein, that is to say, the rein whose action is most intense. A horse whose body is bent has much less chance of resisting and becomes more receptive to the action of the aids. When changing hands in the circle (changing the direction of rotation), the rider places his horse on one rein and then the other, so that when it subsequently moves forward in a straight line, it will respond equally well to both of them. The trot and canter are the most effective gaits in which to apply these actions of the aids; the walk much less so, because the impulsion is too weak. On the other hand, it is at the halt and the rein-back that the horse tries most obstinately to evade the action of the reins.

If the horse gets behind the bit, it decreases the pace. In this event, the rider's reaction should be an energetic urging forward with the legs, which obliges the horse to extend itself and thus to return to the rider's hand. In no case should the rider attempt to re-establish the contact by pulling back with his hands. The correct contact should always be sought and found from back to front. Correct equitation is impossible if this contact is not permanently maintained.

The horse is well in hand when it maintains an appropriate contact at every gait, at every pace, and at every change of gait, pace, and direction, as well as during the halt.

Here again there exists no universal model showing how a horse should hold itself to be well in hand, no diagram of a position that one should try to copy. The horse's head and neck should remain within certain limits in order for the reins to act correctly and for the animal to respond appropriately. The rider's preoccupation should be to maintain them within these limits. Aside from these generalities, the posture (silhouette) of a horse that is well in hand depends above all on its individual conformation.

The *weight aids* are an important element of equitation in that they can be employed passively or actively according to the circumstances, in order to complement the other aids and to coordinate their combined actions.

A horse that is on the aids finds itself, so to speak, enclosed in a frame created by the actions of the legs, reins, and weight—behind, in front, and on both sides. Only under these conditions is it possible for the rider to balance his horse.

A horse is *balanced* when it assumes a posture which aligns its center of gravity to the burden constituted by the rider's weight, and which is adapted to the kind of movement as well as to the nature of the ground.

In order to sit in equilibrium during short gaits, that is, in order to align himself with the horse's center of gravity, the rider must produce in the horse a posture that is in harmony with his own position in the saddle by inducing the animal to displace its center of gravity toward the rear under the burden—in other words, he must balance the horse.

There are two somewhat different ways of accomplishing this:

1. by what is called collection, or gathering the horse;
2. by what is termed the "natural method."

Collection is obtained by the action of the appropriate aids. The horse, already perfectly placed on the aids, is driven forward against the supporting reins with the *active* co-operation of the weight aids, and in this way is compressed from back to front. The animal thus finds itself obliged to engage its hind legs, which are increasingly flexed, well underneath the body and at the same time to raise its head and flex its neck, all of which shortens its posture. In order to strengthen his leg and weight actions, the rider always uses a full seat, first at a collected trot, then at a collected canter, and finally at a walk, which is the most difficult gait in which to collect a horse.

The driving action of the legs assumes great importance. A shortening of the horse, that is, a displacement to the rear of its center of gravity, produces a sufficiently effective change in the distribution of weight *only* if it is accompanied by a correspondingly more forward placement of the hind legs. (The result is that the horse's stride becomes less flat and covers less ground, and becomes high and short instead.) The driving action of the rider's legs not only maintains an indispensable forward movement and prevents an exaggerated shortening of the horse, but also produces a modification of posture from back to front and consequently makes the spine take a position sloping toward the rear. At the same time, it results in a light but steady support by the reins due to the fact that, the more the weight is placed on the hindquarters, the lighter is the support by the reins. (Conversely, the more the weight is placed on the forehand, as with the race horse, the stronger must be the rein support.)

If the horse's gaits are getting irregular, if they are devoid of impulsion or are even contracted or tense, it is a sign that the collection has been undertaken prematurely. In this case, the horse should be permitted to relax by moving forward more freely, and the collection should be resumed only when the animal is perfectly supple and responsive to the actions of the aids.

In this way the rider obtains a shortening of the horse, which is characterized by a higher head and neck carriage as well as by a more pronounced flexing of the poll and neck. The horse is then said to be "*gathered.*" The more the horse is collected, the more its center of gravity is displaced to the rear, the more its hind legs are engaged underneath its body, and the more its shortening is accentuated. This posture permits the rider to sit in equilibrium during short gaits, that is, when a greater share of the total weight must be carried by the hind legs; it also permits the horse more easily to carry the rider (now seated above its center of gravity), lending its movements greater sureness, suppleness, and impulsion. However, it requires of the rider a very complete control over his horse.

The *natural method* is based on the theory that a horse will seek its own balance, without the need of any particular intervention by the rider or the aids. The animal is faced with increasingly difficult tests in different kinds of movements and over varied terrain, and thus progressively adapts itself, in other words, succeeds in balancing itself.

The rider uses his aids only as they may be necessary in order to maintain his horse in the gait, rhythm, and direction he desires. In particular, he should adjust his seat (weight action) *passively* to the horse's balance, as influenced by the kind of movement and the nature of the ground. By riding frequently over extremely varied terrain and by constantly changing the gait, rhythm, and direction (stopping and backing), he will obtain a shortening of the horse and an increased flexion of the hind legs underneath its body in a degree that is perfectly adequate for balancing the horse during cross-country equestrian sports.

But for many riding-school gaits, and particularly for high-school dressage, the balance obtained by this method is insufficient. It is very difficult for the rider to discover any natural means, aside from the action of the aids, which oblige the horse to accomplish these movements, even though a horse will often execute them of its own accord when it is at liberty. Even if the rider were able to find the means to produce some of these movements naturally, he would be unable to utilize them in a sustained manner and to subordinate them to his will. And so the natural method can never result in a perfect mastery over the horse, and an animal schooled in this manner will always remain more independent. However, this independence is, for many of the horse's movements, not only inevitable, but desirable. The rider should take it into account, but at the same time he should direct, influence, and utilize it effectively.

On the other hand, it has been proven that a horse trained in this way is more clever across country (because of its more independent adaptability) than is a horse that has only been collected in the riding ring. It is a practical kind of schooling which, when the animal is on the aids and also moves forward willingly and with impulsion, is perfectly able to prepare the horse for all ordinary riding activities.

Unless there is a particular reason to develop a specialized horse, trained more or less exclusively for school equitation (high-school dressage), jumping (show jumping), or cross-country riding (hunting, racing), an all-around horse should be equally trained in all of these fields and thus acquire the greatest possible versatility. Such a horse should remain in balance both at all the ordinary gaits and when coping with the ordinary problems of varied terrain and obstacles. It should be able to be balanced by collection for work in the riding ring at shortened gaits, and be equally able to be balanced by the natural method for riding across country and for jumping obstacles. In other words, it always should be capable of being placed in a suitable posture. In these conditions, the rider employs his weight actively or passively, but he also uses the other aids, according to the situation, the circumstances, and the goal in view.

There exists no model indicating the exact posture a horse should assume when executing a certain movement, and such a thing never can exist. The horse's posture is only a means of attaining a precise goal, and it is determined by the particular goal. Disregarding for the moment the differences of physical conformation, the posture of a balanced horse should be completely different at a racing gallop, a middle trot, and when performing the levade of high-school dressage. These differences of posture are expressed externally by the extent to which the hind legs come under the body, by the ensuing relative raising of the forehand, and by the resulting position of the head and neck; and these different postures produce all of the different stages of balance that a horse can adopt underneath its rider (Fig. 20).

5. *Intractable Horses*

A horse may be regarded as intractable when it refuses to submit to the rider's will. Most often this is the result of unreasonable, inconsistent, or premature demands which cause the animal to lose confidence and incite it to revolt. However, *only a horse that is not well in hand is able to rebel.*

A good rider never furnishes an occasion for the horse to manifest opposition. He plans the lessons in a logical, clear, and comprehensible sequence, always well within the animal's physical limitations, so that the horse is hardly aware of the increasing difficulty and never becomes upset. But if he is dealing with a horse that has already become stubborn, the rider must avail himself of every possible means in order to emerge victorious from the

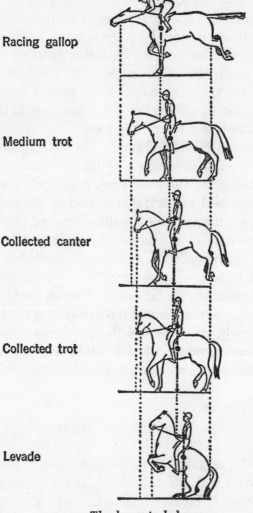

Racing gallop

Medium trot

Collected canter

Collected trot

Levade

FIG. 20. *The horse in balance.*

struggle that is bound to ensue. If he is able to discover the cause, he can usually succeed in restoring the animal's confidence. In no case should a rider lead back to the stable a horse who might be under the impression that it has had its own way, for what was until then merely a seed that might have been destroyed grows into a weapon that the horse will try to wield against the rider at every opportunity. In this way, one may end up with a "vicious" horse who, due to its excellent memory, can no longer be re-habilitated, or only with the greatest difficulty.

Snatching the reins away from the rider is a defense against the rider's hands. The horse gets on the bit and tries to tear the reins out of the rider's hands by jerking with its head and neck. These jerks can be so strong, particularly when the rider is taken by surprise, that they can unseat an inexperienced horseman.

By a particularly firm seat and the driving action of the aids, the rider should anticipate the horse's movement and set his hands so solidly that the animal, in trying to pull away the reins, tears its own mouth. But at the very next instant, the hands should again become soft and light, in order to induce the horse to resume a normal contact with the bit.

Throwing the head is another form of opposition to the action of the reins, and it must be combated just as in the preceding case. The driving aids play a particularly important role, because this resistance is generally accompanied by a slackening of pace. In the most serious cases, it may be advantageous to use a martingale, which facilitates the supporting action of the reins at the critical moment by limiting the extent to which the horse can throw its head.

Rearing, in which the horse rises on its hind legs, stems from the animal's desire to escape from a hand that is disagreeable and often brutal, or else from too severe a bit. This defense is often employed by horses whose hindquarters are powerful and low, frequently in reaction to an unreasonable demand on the part of the rider, and thus from desperation.

A horse can rear only when standing still and, in order to lift its forehand, it must throw its head up high. By urging the animal forward and by suitably burdening the forehand at the proper moment, the rearing can be prevented. If the proper moment has already passed, you can try to bring the horse to hand again by turning it to the more flexible side, at the same time urging it forward.

In no case should both reins be pulled, for this would only give the horse a prop, permitting it to rear more easily and, in certain circumstances, might result in its coming over backward.

Running away occurs with animals who wish to escape the rider's actions, especially rein actions, by means of flight. Often the cause is too sharp a bit, and the change to a rubber snaffle in such a case frequently accomplishes miracles.

A tactful rider never allows a situation to reach the point where the horse runs away. He prevents the animal from bolting by yielding with the reins in time and by trying to calm it. Once the horse has gotten out of hand, it can no longer be restrained by pulling on the reins. In such a case the rider should, with a strong, steady pull on one rein, try to make the animal turn in a circle to the more flexible side and eventually get it to come to a stop by gradually reducing the diameter of the circle. If he does not succeed in turning the horse, however, and the terrain happens to be appropriate, he can simply let it run until the horse has had enough of this furious pace, and then oblige it to continue to gallop as a form of punishment. On such occasions a couple of pricks by the spurs are quite in order, for they will leave a frightening impression in the horse's memory.

It is always unwise to saw on the horse's mouth with the snaffle, and the results obtained are never worth while.

Kicking when under saddle is frequently caused by exuberance in the pleasure of movement, such as after jumping an obstacle, when the horse avails itself of the freedom of its head and back. But it is also very often a reaction to an ill-fitting saddle, a girth that is badly adjusted or too tight, an inopportune use of the spurs, or, finally, a warning to another horse that approaches too close from behind. This vice can be eliminated immediately by eliminating its cause. On the other hand, it will only be aggravated if the rider, through incomprehension, either takes no suitable action or, at the other extreme, behaves brutally toward the horse.

A rather frequent occurrence, especially with mares, is *excessive sensitivity at being saddled or girthed,* often due to a badly placed saddle or to tightening the girth too soon. In this case, the greatest precaution must be taken while saddling the horse, attaching the girth very loosely at first and only tightening it later, after the horse has been led about for a while.

Bucking is an attempt to unseat the rider. The horse rounds its back like a cat, lowers its head, and jumps in place off all four feet. If the rider succeeds in pulling the animal's head up energetically and in urging it forward, he usually succeeds in breaking this resistance and avoids being thrown.

When I was a young horseman, I learned at my own expense, due to a misunderstanding, that such an incident may in fact well conclude in this undignified manner. It was at the cavalry school. We had to ride some recently arrived horses that day. I was assigned a big bay whose appearance did not inspire me with great confidence. Hardly had I slid into the saddle when the animal began to buck with unexpected violence. I stuck to the saddle as best I could. Our instructor, from whom we usually received commands only in the form of criticism, such as "Raise the head," "Lower the hands," "Pull back the leg," and so forth, watched me tranquilly for a moment and then ordered, "Raise the head!" I raised my head, but undoubtedly not sufficiently, so great was my preoccupation with my predicament, for again I received, in an even more commanding tone, the order *"Raise the head!"* I did my best to obey, but, when the instructor called out for the third time, "RAISE THE HEAD!" I found myself unable to comply. . . . I was already on the ground. It was only then that I learned that the instructor wished me to raise the horse's head and not my own.

A *herd-bound* horse refuses to move away from the other horses and sometimes even refuses to move away from the stable. This vice originates in large part from the horse's native herd instinct, and, ordinarily, it is not difficult to correct by suitable training, which emphasizes frequent rides alone during which the rider exercises great patience and kindness (rewards), but also great firmness (punishment) if necessary.

Shying sometimes arises from an excess of playfulness. In this case, the horse ceases to shy when it has used up its excess energy in normal exercise. But in other cases, shying is caused by defective eyesight, a weakness which is often combined with a timid character and should be considered quite a serious flaw in a riding horse. There is no radically effective means of combating it. All that can be done is to try to calm the animal with kind words, to turn its head away from the object which frightens it, and to urge it forward with sufficient energy.

Here is an example of shying provoked by a weakness of eyesight. One beautiful moonlit night, I was riding along a chalky lane that was almost as bright as in the daytime. Every fifteen or twenty yards there were trees which cast their shadows on the road. My mare, whom I intended to train with show jumping in view, but whom I already suspected of having poor eyesight, jumped every shadow as if it were an obstacle. It was absolutely impossible for me to get her to place her foot on one of these dark strips. All my efforts were in vain. She jumped impeccably the shadow of every tree the entire two miles of the way, until we finally reached our destination, both of us dripping with perspiration. Needless to say, after this exhausting experience, I abandoned my idea of training the mare for jumping.

Ticklish horses are abnormally sensitive to physical contact. The extreme cases are very difficult and disagreeable to ride, because they react immediately and violently to every touch—of the leg, the hand, a piece of clothing, etc.—by rounding the back and kicking. Mares are particularly prone to this vice; it is manifested most intensely when they are in heat, and during these periods it can be almost impossible to ride them.

Since this kind of vice is more or less pathological in nature, it is practically impossible to cure.

CHAPTER 3

IN THE RIDING RING

IN THE RIDING RING

Any clear space where the ground is suitable can be used as a riding ring. If the dimensions permit, a *rectangle* may be laid out with the short sides at least twenty meters long and the long sides at least forty, or, if possible, sixty meters long. (This is approximately 66 feet by 131 to 197 feet.) In order to permit working even when the weather is bad, particularly during the winter, an *indoor ring* can be used, with the ground covered by a layer of sawdust. While such a facility offers many advantages, since it eliminates distractions and permits the horses to concentrate better, it should always be remembered that work in the fresh—even cold—outdoor air is much healthier for them. Many respiratory and lung ailments develop as a result of working exclusively in an indoor ring.

Every riding ring is composed of two *long walls* or *sides,* two *short* ones, and four corners. The path running the length of the four walls is called the *outside track,* and there is a second one, the *inside track,* three strides (say, thirty inches) to the inside of the walls. The side of the rider and horse that is on the inside of the ring is called the "inside," the other being the "outside." And so we will speak of a foot, a rein, a leg, and so forth, as being either inside or outside. When riding around the ring clockwise, you are said to be moving *to the right* or *on the right hand;* in the opposite sense, counterclockwise, you are moving *to the left* or *on the left hand*.

The *large circle* or *volte* has as its diameter the width of the ring. It can thus be performed at both ends of the ring, where it is bounded by one short wall and two long ones, as well as in the center of the ring. The *small circle* or *volte* has a diameter of six strides and can take place in any part of the ring. Two tangent circles make a *figure eight*. A series of successive half circles forms a *serpentine*.

To make a *change of hand* is to change the direction of rotation in the ring or in the large circle. When riding around the ring, a change of direction is made by passing through the center of the ring, through the diagonals of the ring; or by a *half turn* or *half volte*. In the large circle or volte, the change of hand is made in the very center of the circle; when riding on two circles, it is made when passing from one to the other; but in both cases, it is made on a line in the form of an S (Fig. 21).

If there are many riders in the ring, they can move in *single file*, one behind the other, with or without a space between them; they can move *individually;* or *at random* (in no particular formation). Beginners, however, should start by riding in a close single file (perhaps with the reins lying knotted on the horse's neck), the column being led by the first rider. In this way the others have practically no need to intervene in guiding their mounts and can devote all of their attention to their seat or to the general exercises being performed.

Among these different exercises, which should always be chosen in view of the pupil's individual aptitude, the following selection is particularly recommended: 1. *rotating the arms,* which are raised vertically, dropped slowly behind, and then brought vigorously forward again; 2. *rotating the trunk,* with the arms stretched sideways, during which the pupil touches the horse's left hip with the right hand when the rotation is to the right, and touches the horse's right hip with his left hand when rotating to the left; 3. *raising and separating the knees,* while both hands are supported on the cantle; 4. *swinging the lower part of the leg,* which is bent supply forward and backward from the knee; 5. *swinging the*

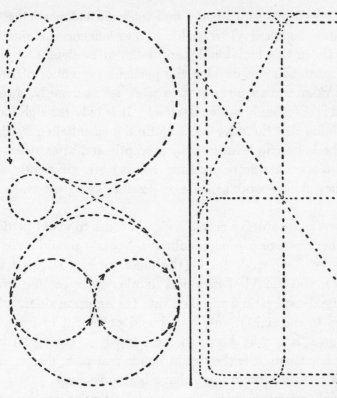

Large circle (volte),
small circle, half
turn, changes of hand
in the circle, change
of circles

The track, the inside
track, and the different
kinds of changes of
hand in the riding ring

FIG. 21. *Riding-school figures.*

feet up and down with supple movements; 6. *rotating the tips of the toes,* which are raised and describe circles toward the outside. The pupils may also be asked to perform all sorts of other movements designed to develop a free and independent seat: touching one part or another of the horse; throwing and picking up objects, etc. However, all of these exercises should be frequently alternated and practiced only during very brief intervals; in between, the riders should always correct their position in the saddle (and to do this, they may hold onto the pommel for a moment).

As soon as the novice has acquired a certain degree of confidence in himself and in his horse, and sufficient independence of seat (balance, suppleness) to enable him to influence his mount, he can begin to ride individually and later, at random. Only individual instruction can develop the particular qualities of each horse and rider and require them to work spontaneously, attentively, and consequently more effectively. It is only through individual training that the rider can acquire the essential equestrian tact and the horse can learn to obey promptly and attentively. In any case, as soon as the riders (and horses) are sufficiently advanced, they should work as little as possible along the walls of the ring.

The riders must observe certain rules in order to avoid getting in each other's way or causing a collision. Nobody should walk or stop when on the outside track (the inner track is reserved for slow work); you should always pass another rider coming from the opposite direction on a specified side (in America, riders generally keep to the right), and you should never cut in front of another horse. If a rider keeps to the left when passing an approaching horseman, it is their right hands that pass, that is, the hands that in earlier times might have borne weapons.

Individual training requires very special attention on the part of the instructor. The promptness and effectiveness of his corrections depend on the keenness of his observation. As far as possible, he should teach, not by simple commands, but by stimulating the intelligence of his pupils, explaining to them what he is asking them to do and what are their faults, making judicious comparisons, and, whenever necessary, giving them a personal demonstration.

Each exercise that the instructor selects for his pupils should be logically adapted to the desired goal, and should develop from the preceding exercises. The rider will learn the right seat, the right feeling, and the ability to influence his horse by putting it through different gaits, by reducing or accelerating the rhythm, by changing directions, by stopping and backing—in short, by influencing the horse according to the goal set forth in each exercise.

1. The Start Forward

The *start forward* (advance) should be preceded by a correct seat on the part of the rider, and a perfectly straight position of the horse.

By means of the driving aids, whose intensity should be in proportion to the animal's degree of sensitivity as well as to the desired gait and rhythm, the hind legs are urged forward underneath the horse's body, which in turn causes a forward displacement of the forelegs. The rider's hands remain passive, that is to say, their function is limited to assuring sufficient contact with the horse's mouth to afford a normal degree of support. As soon as the desired forward movement has been produced, the rider ceases the action of the driving aids, but remains ready to resume action as soon as the horse attempts to reduce the rhythm. The rein aids remain passive, but are ready to become active the moment the horse seeks to increase the rhythm on its own. In time, the rider should acquire so well-developed a sense of these aid actions that the slightest hint that the horse might modify the rhythm sets them into operation automatically. The action of the driving aids is particularly important during forward movements, and its effect should be visible in the horse's entire posture (position of the spine). During schooling, the rider should urge on his mount, once it has had a chance to relax, so that the actual speed is always slightly faster than the horse would choose itself.

The advance is not limited to the transition from immobility to movement, but also includes every transition from one gait or rhythm to a faster one. It is obtained in every case by the driving action of the legs with the appropriate collaboration of the weight aids: the rider urges his horse to increase its speed with his driving aids, and only then does he adjust his seat to the animal's more extended position. In other words, he uses his weight *passively*.

2. *Straightening the Horse*

Straightening the horse is achieved by obliging the hindquarters to follow the forehand in such a way that the hind feet fall on *exactly* the same line as the forefeet. This line may be straight, or it may be curved (when riding on a circle); the horse should always remain on the same track with the forehand as with the hindquarters. If the horse does not remain straight, the result is a deviation toward the outside by either the hindquarters or the forehand. In the first case, the fault can be corrected by the rider's leg on the deviating side while the opposite rein effects a supporting action; in the second case, the rein on the opposite side returns the forehand to the correct track, while the leg on the deviating side restrains. In both cases, care must be taken to maintain a uniform and lively rhythm.

If a horse does not move forward in a straight posture, the cause may be an insufficient or defective action of the rider's aids, or an asymmetrical construction of the horse. This asymmetry may be to the right or to the left; it is due to a natural incurvation of the horse's body, which occurs during its embryonic development in its mother's womb and consists of a one-sided development of its muscular system. The phenomenon is similar to that which causes some people to be left-handed and others right-handed.

This natural *asymmetry* can be felt by the rider in the form of a more or less pronounced stiffness on the right or left side of the horse, and consequently a weaker response to the rein aids applied to the stiff side, and to the leg aids on the opposite side. Such a horse furnishes most of the effort required to perform a particular movement by means of the best-developed part of its body, that is, by its legs—and especially by the hind leg on the stiff side. An unbalanced physical construction is reflected in the horse's position and direction; it takes the form of uneven strides and oblique movements in which the hind legs do not follow the same track as the forelegs.

This fault can and should be corrected by well-chosen and progressive suppling exercises, with the principal purpose of producing flexion in the stiff side, which is most often the right one.

3. *The Halt*

The *retarding movements* (or *parades*), as opposites to the advancing movements, slow down the horse or stop it completely. The two forms are: the half halt and the full halt.

The *half halt* can either shorten the rhythm of a gait or make the horse go into a shorter gait: from the canter to the trot or walk, for example; or from the trot to the walk. The appropriate aids are therefore just the opposite of those used to initiate or accelerate forward movement. First of all, the rider must take a fuller seat, suitable to the desired shortening of the horse, which means that he employs his weight aids *actively*. In order to shorten the horse, he applies a restraining action of the rein aids, and at the same time his legs, placed directly behind the girth, support the hindquarters. These actions oblige the hind legs to adjust to the horse's new (shortened) posture by flexing themselves more strongly and engaging themselves further under the horse's body.

The half halt can also be used to improve the animal's posture within the gait, without any slackening of speed. In this case, the rein aids should support rather than restrain.

The *full halt* should bring the horse to a stop from any gait at all. It is obtained by means of the same aids as the half halt, except that their intensity must be increased until a state of immobility has been achieved. However, the aid actions must be very carefully adapted to the horse's degree of training, for if they are too brutal they can eventually cause damage to the horse's physical structure (joints) and even to its character.

A halt is faultless only when it is performed, while the horse is well on the bit, by a shortening of the posture (weight distribution)—in other words, when it is performed with suppleness by all four legs—and when the horse stops in a perfectly straight position (Fig. 22). The distance required to come to a halt depends

Right

Wrong

Wrong

FIG. 22. *A halt is faultless only when it is performed, while the horse is well on the bit, by a shortening of the posture.*

on the original gait, the rider's skill, and especially on the horse's degree of training. It should be immediate when executed at a walk; it should take place after three strides from a trot, and after six strides from a canter. When the rider and horse are both perfectly schooled, it can be immediate from any gait.

The halt merits particular attention from the point of view of the rider's training. The pupil should be warned that when stretching the small of his back he should not hollow it nor lean the upper part of his body behind the vertical, but should keep his torso perfectly erect. The consequence of leaning backward is that the horse, in order to escape the increased burden on the hindquarters, often leans more heavily on the bit. Leaning forward impairs the action of the aids.

SCHOOL RIDING 5. Shoulder in to the left.

SCHOOL RIDING   6. Travers to the right.

JUMPING   7. On a longeing rein.

JUMPING   8. Over a series of obstacles.

4. *The Turn in Place,*
on the Forehand and on the Hindquarters

The *turn in place* has hardly any practical value at all, and is useful only in teaching the rider and horse the lateral action of the aids, after they have already become familiar with the driving and restraining actions.

During all the exercises requiring a lateral position or a lateral bending of the horse's body, the side toward which the horse is placed or bent is called the "inside," and the opposite one the "outside." It is therefore possible for the inside of the horse to be turned toward the outside of the riding ring, and thus to be in contradiction with the usual meaning of these terms.

There are two forms of turns in place: 1. the turn on the forehand, which is performed around the shoulder; and 2. the turn on the hindquarters, which is performed around the croup.

The *turn on the forehand* is a rotating movement in which the horse turns the hindquarters around the forehand, with the inside forefoot acting as the pivot. It can be a turn to the left or to the right, of 90° or 180°, although a lesser degree is quite adequate for schooling purposes (Fig. 23).

If, for example, the turn is to be made to the right, the rider takes the preliminary action of turning the horse's head with the right rein slightly toward the right (just enough for him to be able to see half of the horse's right eye), then he acts with his right leg, placed a hand's width behind the girth, to push the hindquarters sideways, step by step. In the meantime, his left leg, placed behind the girth, exerts a restraining action in order to prevent too rapid a lateral displacement or any backward displacement of the hindquarters; and the left rein, by a light supporting action, guards against a deviation of the left shoulder. When turning to the left, all of these actions are simply reversed.

If the horse moves forward while turning, it should be restrained. If it moves backward (the more serious fault), it must immediately be driven forward in a straight line and only after-

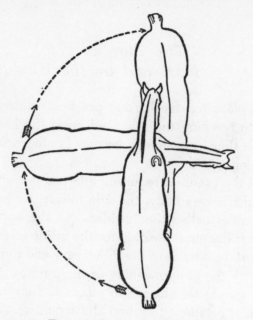

FIG. 23. *Turn on the forehand to the right.*

ward should the turning be resumed. The movement should be performed step by step, so that the rider is able to interrupt it at any moment. An excessively vigorous turning by the hindquarters is a very bad fault.

As schooling progresses, the lateral position (bending) of the horse's head will become less and less pronounced, so that it will eventually become practically unnecessary.

The *turn on the hindquarters* is a rotation by the forehand around the hindquarters, with the inside hind leg acting as the pivot. It too can be performed either to the right or to the left and can measure up to 180° (a full turn) (Fig. 24). Though closely related to the turn on the forehand, it has special value as a preparatory exercise to the work on two tracks and should be taught immediately before it.

When the turn on the hindquarters is performed to the right, the rider uses the right rein to bend the horse slightly to the right until he can see half of the animal's right eye, and at the same time he shifts his weight onto his right buttock. While the right rein

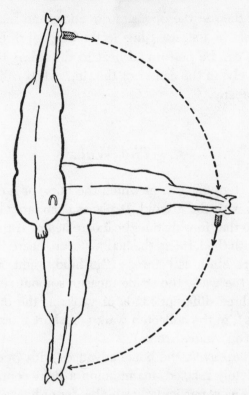

FIG. 24. *Turn on the hindquarters to the right.*

then initiates the turn, the left leg, placed a hand's width to the rear of the girth, guides the turn step by step around the hindquarters, at the same time preventing any deviation of the hind legs toward the outside. Simultaneously, the left rein prevents a deviation of the left shoulder by means of a light supporting action, and the right leg exerts a restraining action in order to prevent the right (inside) hind foot from moving either backward or sideways. The turn to the left is produced in the same manner by the action of the opposite aids.

By practicing turns in place, the rider acquires a clear feeling of the action of the aids as well as of their harmonious and effective combination, which is most important. He should eventually achieve such a high degree of control that he is able to stop his horse at will, to make it perform a definite number of steps in turning around the forehand or the hindquarters, to the right or to the left, then in the opposite direction, and finally to move it forward again in a straight line in the original direction. These turns in place can be performed next to the riding-ring walls or, just as effectively, in the center of the ring, when riding individually or in company.

5. *The Walk*

The *walk* is a stepping gait in which the horse at no time loses a direct contact with the ground. It places each lateral pair of feet successively so that four distinct beats are heard. If the movement commences with the left leg, the hoofbeats are heard in the following order: left hind, left fore, right hind, right fore, and so forth. During the walk, the stride measures about six feet.

There are three different kinds of walk: 1. the ordinary walk (on long reins); 2. the collected walk (on short reins); 3. the extended walk (on yielded reins).

In the *ordinary walk*, the horse advances with free, even, long strides, completely relaxed, maintaining a light contact with the bit. This gait is most particularly suitable for ordinary riding (over varied terrain, during long hacks) and is consequently the most frequently employed. The speed is about one hundred meters per minute (just under four miles an hour)* (Fig. 25).

In the *collected walk*, the horse is gathered (collected) by the driving aids, with the reins supporting and the weight aids active. The stride is shorter. This gait is used only during dressage (in the riding ring) (Fig. 25).

In the *extended walk*, the horse moves forward without any support from the reins and is therefore able to stretch out its head and neck in complete freedom. As a result its steps, activated by the driving aids, should be extremely free and extended. Since this is the gait that is least tiring to the horse, it is the one that is used during rest periods in order to permit the horse as well as the rider to recover from the fatigue of previous efforts (Fig. 25).

* The various cavalries have established rates of speed that are all virtually identical.

Walk on short reins

Walk on long reins

Walk on yielded reins

FIG. 25. *The walk.*

6. *The Trot*

The *trot* is a springing gait in which the horse moves its two diagonal pairs of legs alternately, so that only two beats are heard, in this succession: the right hind simultaneously with the left fore, then the left hind simultaneously with the right fore. After each strike there is an interval of suspension during which the feet do not touch the ground. This gait is normally faster than the walk, and the length of stride can exceed twenty feet.

There are four different kinds of trot, depending on the horse's posture and consequently on the length of stride: 1. the ordinary trot (working trot); 2. the collected trot (short trot); 3. the medium trot (strong trot); and 4. the extended trot.

In the *ordinary trot*, the horse moves with its body posture free and unconstrained, and this is therefore the most useful rhythm of the trotting gait. It is also used in the riding ring, in which case it may be a little more energetic and shorter. But it is particularly suitable when the gait must be sustained for a long period of time, and so it is generally used for cross-country riding and during long hacks. The speed should be about two hundred meters per minute (say, eight miles per hour) (Fig. 26).

Collected trot (sitting trot)

Ordinary trot (posting trot)

Extended trot (posting trot)

FIG. 26. *The trot.*

In the *collected trot*, the horse is urged forward against the supporting hands by a stronger action of the driving aids, so that its hind legs are increasingly flexed and engaged further underneath its body, while its head and neck are raised higher; the horse is, in other words, collected. The strides become shorter, but they should also be more vigorous and higher. This is the gait that lends itself best to gathering (collecting) the horse, but it should not be maintained for too long a time and should always be alternated with freer paces. The collected trot is used exclusively for dressage (in the riding ring) (Fig. 26).

The speed is somewhat less than two hundred meters per minute, the exact rate depending upon the horse's degree of collection. It is possible for the horse to be so highly collected that this gait is performed practically in place, like the "piaffer" of high-school dressage.

In the *medium trot,* the horse should be more extended, and this is possible only if the rider urges it forward and if his hands follow the horse's neck as it stretches out. The strides become vigorous and long, without the animal's leaning too heavily on the bit. The medium trot, on the one hand, stimulates the horse's desire to move forward and develops the propulsive force of the hindquarters; on the other hand, it strengthens the rider's seat and improves his aid actions. This trot is used only for schooling, and exclusively in the riding ring. The speed is three hundred meters per minute (about eleven miles per hour).

In the *extended trot,* the rider's driving aids become even stronger, the hands follow the horse as it extends itself and seeks a stronger support from the bit. The strides should be even, vigorous, and long. This is consequently the fastest form of trot and should be used only during rather brief intervals when working on the springy ground of a riding ring (Fig. 26).

There are also two further variants of the trot, depending on the rider's seat: 1. the sitting trot; and 2. the rising trot (posting).

In the *sitting trot,* the rider is constantly supported on his two buttocks and sits in the saddle with the small of the back supple and erect; in other words, he assumes a full seat. His body should follow the motion of the horse—or, rather, accompany it through a relaxed seat. The force of the shocks he receives depends partly on the physical conformation of the horse, but mostly on its posture. When a horse is well balanced and its posture is adapted to the burden it carries, the rider should sit vertically above the horse's center of gravity. In this way the horse is able to carry its burden comfortably and can produce a gait that is natural, relaxed, and consequently supple and vigorous. In other words, when the horse is *balanced*, the rider finds it possible to be *seated in equilibrium*, in a supple and easy manner. However, when the horse is not well balanced, the rider who uses a full seat overburdens the hindquarters (the rear arm of the lever), and the movements of the quarters become even stronger as the rider is further removed from the center of gravity. This burden hampers the horse in its weight-carrying effort and in its impulsion; its movements become more or less stiff, they are more or less contracted and faltering, sometimes heavy and sometimes hurried and violent. Under these conditions, the rider feels the shocks from the horse's back in a very intense and disagreeable manner.

In the collected trot, the rider can be in equilibrium only when he is in a sitting position. The same is true of the ordinary trot, when performed in the riding ring as a training exercise, for only when the rider is in a full seat can the horse be gathered and maintained in this collected posture. Furthermore, the sitting trot plays an exceptionally important role in the training of novice riders. It is only by sitting to the trot (sometimes without stirrups) that they can acquire correct balance and a correct seat, as well as subtle feelings and refined actions. The sitting trot supples the muscles and limbs, strengthens the small of the back, and develops its elasticity. However, care should be taken not to overdo this exercise, for if it is too prolonged, all the rider's muscles become tired, tense, and stiffened. The periods should therefore never be too long and always alternated with work in a more comfortable seat and at a livelier pace.

In the *rising trot* (*posting*), the movements of both horse and rider are facilitated. The rider rises slightly above the saddle from his knees, so that his seat is in the air at every second hoofbeat. Thus he is in the saddle during only one hoofbeat out of every two that the horse makes as it alternately places its two diagonal pairs of feet on the ground. In America, when the rider is seated in the saddle when the right foreleg is on the ground (which simultaneously burdens the diagonal hind leg), the rider is said to rise or post on the right diagonal. In Europe, he is said to rise or post on the right leg. A change of diagonal (or leg) is made either by remaining in the saddle during two successive hoofbeats, or by resting on the stirrups during two beats. The first method is preferable, because it maintains a better contact with the horse.

During cross-country riding and long hacks, the diagonal should be changed about every half mile. In the riding ring, however, the custom varies according to the country. For example, the Germans, French, and Swiss usually require the rising trot to be on the outside foreleg, thus on the inside hind leg; others (for example, the Swedes, Russians, and Poles) recommend posting on the inside foreleg, thus on the outside hind leg. The latter custom is more justifiable, because when trotting on the outside hind leg the horse is able to advance the inside hind leg further underneath its body, it being less burdened, and the horse can therefore flex itself better. Furthermore, since the rider is sitting as the inside hind leg advances, he can drive more effectively and thus urge the horse to advance this leg even further. In certain countries, however, there are no rules at all concerning changing the leg or diagonal during the trot.

During the rising trot, the rider should follow the horse's movements with suppleness, which he accomplishes by leaning forward, but not to an exaggerated degree. The small of the back should never "sag" to the rear, but should constantly remain erect. The knees and calves, placed flat and slightly tighter, remain in place, the knees acting as points of support and rotation, and the legs constantly prepared to provide the necessary impulsion.

The posting trot enables the rider to follow the horse's movements and remain in equilibrium during the faster trotting paces. Consequently, this seat is frequently used with the working (ordinary) trot in the riding ring and always when the working trot is performed over varied terrain or during long hacks; it is the seat that should always be used for the medium trot and the extended trot, in order to offer the horse the possibility of assuming a more extended posture.

Every beginner should learn to post as well as to make a change of diagonals. A most worth-while exercise consists in schooling young riders in the rising trot without stirrups.*

7. *The Canter and Gallop*

The *canter*** and *gallop* are visibly springing gaits, involving a definite phase of suspension. They may be *on the right lead* or *on the left lead.* In the first case, the movement begins with the left hind leg, then the right hind and the left fore strike the ground almost simultaneously, and last of all the right fore, which becomes the "leading leg" and gives its name to the particular kind of canter or gallop. For the left lead, the footfall is reversed: it starts with the right hind, continues with the simultaneous strikes of the left hind and the right fore, and finally by the strike of the left fore. The last then becomes the leading leg. Following each of these strike sequences, there is an interval of suspension during which none of the feet touches the ground.

Consequently, three beats are normally heard during the canter, the second one being slightly more prolonged than the others. Only when the canter is short and lazy (with the hind legs brought insufficiently underneath the horse's body), or when the gallop is carried to its maximum speed (racing gallop), does a certain interval of time separate the strikes of the diagonal pair of legs (the second phase). In the first case, the result is a faulty four-beat canter; in the second case, the interval becomes still longer and there are only two drawn-out beats made by the striking of the two hind legs and the two forelegs.

* This exercise, as well as jumping without stirrups, requires a firm grip with the knees and legs and should therefore be performed with the heels held low and the tips of the toes raised. In all the other exercises without stirrups, where the purpose is to develop a relaxed seat (balance), the legs and feet should hang freely.
** On the European continent this gait is always called a "gallop" no matter what its speed, and "canter" is used only for the slow gallop of a race horse.

The gallop is the horse's fastest gait, and the stride can exceed nine yards.

In the riding ring, you should canter to the right on the right lead and to the left on the left lead. If the lead is reversed, contrary to the rider's intention, so that the leading leg is the outside foreleg, it is called a "false lead." During a false canter, the rider feels a jolt under the outside buttock, and his outside shoulder is violently thrown forward at each leap; the horse is attempting to make him shift his seat. However, the rider should never look down at the horse's feet in order to verify that the animal is on a false lead; he should learn to recognize it by its feeling.

The gait is also faulty when the horse canters on the right lead behind and on the left with the forelegs, or vice versa. In this case, the horse is said to be "disunited." At this kind of canter, the rider feels the disagreeable disunited movement of the horse most distinctly, due to the fact that the feet on one side are unnaturally spread apart and on the other side they are too close together; a fall can even result from this uncomfortable situation.

To *"strike off" at a canter*, the horse should first of all be placed in the position appropriate to the gait: to the right for a canter on the right lead, to the left for a canter on the left lead. In order to strike off on the right lead, the rider turns the animal's head with the right rein sufficiently toward the right for him to see half of the horse's right eye; at the same time, he supports with the left rein so that the animal does not leave the track, which may be either straight or curved (when riding on a circle). The right (inside) leg is placed against the girth; the left (outside) leg is a hand's width behind the girth and gives the horse a slight longitudinal flexion around the inside leg. In this way the correct position for striking off into a canter on the right lead is obtained (Fig. 27).

If the horse were standing still in this position, its natural reaction would be to set out at a walk or trot under the rider's impulsion, then to accelerate the speed at the rider's urging and finally to go into a precipitate and disorderly kind of canter. However, we are not interested in going *faster*, but in producing

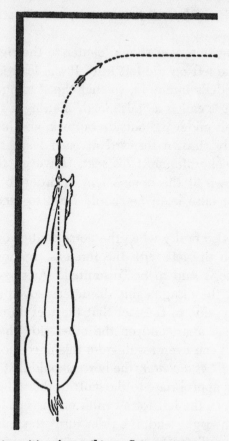

FIG. 27. *Correct position for striking off into a canter on the right lead.*

a specific gait that corresponds to a definite succession of well-regulated hoofbeats. Therefore, when striking off into a canter from the walk or trot, the horse must modify the *sequence* of hoofbeats in the appropriate manner, without previously accelerating the *rhythm* in the slightest degree; or, if it strikes off from a standstill, it should establish the canter immediately.

In order to achieve this aim, the rider displaces his weight so that he rests a bit more heavily on the right (inside) seat bone. (The full seat is always used when striking off.) By supporting with the reins (while maintaining the lateral position of the horse's head) and by stretching the small of his back (active weight aids), he prevents the horse from accelerating the rhythm (or

from going into a walk or trot, when striking off from a standstill);
and he drives it forward with the inside leg, while the other leg
exerts a restraining (holding) action. During this action of the
aids, the rider's right (inside) leg drives the right (inside) hind
leg forward, while at the same time the support exerted by the
left (outside) rein limits the forward thrust of the horse's left
(outside) hind leg. The horse is thus induced to start the sequence
of hoofbeats for the canter on the right lead, and to strike off into
a canter on this lead. But in order to perform the first leap of the
canter, the horse must stretch out its head and neck to a certain
extent; it is therefore important for the hands, which previously
supported, to become immediately passive the moment the horse
extends its head and neck, and to follow the forward movement
of the horse's mouth while maintaining a supple contact.

- When the horse strikes off into a canter, and in fact during all
the time it performs this gait, the rider must take great care to see
that it is kept quite straight, which means that the hindquarters
should follow the forehand very exactly and not fall to the inside.
This fault can be corrected by the inside (driving) leg and the
inside rein. From the moment his horse starts to canter and during
all the time it performs this gait, the rider should place the
horse so that he has the feeling that the forehand is slightly directed toward the inside (the shoulder-in); in this way, the forehand will be exactly in line with the hindquarters. On the other
hand, it is a very bad fault to displace the forehand toward the
inside by a lateral pressure of the outside rein against the horse's
neck, because the correct position will be lost without the rider's
having succeeded in straightening the horse.

The inside leg, on the girth, produces impulsion; it also guards
against the hindquarters' deviating from the track. The outside
leg, on the rear of the girth, exerts a restraining action and supports the forward movement of the horse. At the moment of striking off into the canter, the inside leg should, as a general rule, act
more strongly than the outside one; however, it is impossible to
say in advance how much stronger its action should be, or to
what degree the rider should squeeze with both legs. This depends upon the horse and its degree of training; if it is well

schooled, incredibly delicate aids are sufficient. The outside leg should keep the horse slightly flexed, but avoid at all costs placing the hindquarters in a crooked position, that is, making them deviate from the track toward the inside (position of the travers).

If a change of lead has to be made, as may be the case when the horse has made a false start or changed leads on its own initiative, or when the rider wishes to make a change of hand in the riding ring, he must first return to the original gait and straighten the horse. When the animal is once again placed in the correct position, he can strike off again into the new lead. When riding in single file, the rider should first close in on the heels of the horse preceding him. This is a *simple change of lead at the canter.*

The half halt during the canter (shortening the rhythm) is normally produced by simultaneous actions of both reins. However, this general rule does not apply when passing from the canter to a trot or walk, or from the canter to a full halt. In these cases, the rider should pull the inside rein just a little bit sooner than the outside rein, at the moment when the inside forefoot is placed on the ground; in this way the sequence of canter strikes is interrupted and the interval of suspension will not take place; the horse places its outside hind foot on the ground and at this moment it can be brought to a halt as desired by acting with the outside rein. The horse will easily understand these aids and the execution of the halt will be supple and precise.

Work at the canter should start as early as possible during the rider's training. It is the best means of developing a sense of balance and of the correct seat. The canter usually has more rhythm and is consequently more agreeable a gait than the trot. However, at the beginning the instructor will often find it necessary to help a horse strike off into a canter either by using his voice or even a whip; but since this causes the horse to be driven into the gait, the canter should, in this case, be started from a trot. As soon as the rider has acquired a certain degree of independence, he should be asked to strike into the canter on his own. The most favorable preconditions occur on a circle, or in a corner of the riding ring when coming from a long wall to a short one, because the horse's inflexion at these moments facilitates placing it in the correct strike-off position. Later on, the rider should be asked to strike into a canter at a gradually increased distance from the corner, until he is finally able to do it on the straight. It is much easier for the rider as well as for the horse to learn this exercise when starting from a walk, because the correct sequence of hoof-beats for the canter can be obtained more easily and more smoothly when starting from the hoofbeat pattern of the walk than from that of the trot. It is also much easier at a walk to prevent the horse from accelerating the rhythm before the strike-off —in other words, to prevent it from breaking into a trot from a walk—than it is to maintain a short trot.

There are four different kinds of canter, depending upon the horse's posture and consequently on the length of stride: 1. the ordinary canter (working canter); 2. the collected canter (short canter); 3. the medium canter (strong canter); and 4. the extended canter (hand gallop).

In the *ordinary canter*, the horse's posture should be natural and its movements calm and free. The rhythm is 225 meters per minute (eight miles per hour); it is particularly suited for schooling exercises (full seat) in the riding ring, but much less so for work out of doors.

In the *collected canter*, the horse is urged by means of the driving aids to engage its hind legs farther forward underneath its body, and to this end the reins (particularly the outside rein) should support (half halt). The horse is thus placed in a collected posture which results in moving the center of gravity backward and in making the animal's action shorter and higher. The rhythm is less than 225 meters per minute, and depends upon the horse's degree of collection; it can even become a "canter in place" (high-school dressage). The best preparatory exercises for this gait are frequent circles (during which the horse should bend its body and engage its inside hind leg well forward underneath the body), as well as halts and striking off into the canter. On the other hand, it is a mistake to try to shorten the horse by pulling back on the reins instead of by urging the hindquarters forward. The quarters would drag behind and the gait would be lazy and lack impulsion. The result would be a "four-beat" canter.

In the collected canter, which is used only in the schooling ring, the rider must take a full seat in order to be in equilibrium, since the center of gravity has been displaced toward the rear (Fig. 28). His body should be perfectly erect, though the alternating up-and-down movement of the forehand and hindquarters will give the impression of leaning alternately forward and backward to the rhythm of the canter.

In the *medium canter*, the horse moves at a speed of 333 meters per minute (twelve miles per hour) and should therefore assume a longer posture. The forehand, which becomes lower, requires firmer support; and the strides, which should be supple and even, become longer and cover a greater amount of ground. The increased force of the hindquarters obliges the horse to use its back with increased activity and so, in order to sit in equilibrium, the rider must follow the movement (the horse's center of gravity being displaced toward the front) by leaning forward, rather the same as during the rising trot, except that both buttocks remain in the saddle. The medium canter can be practiced in the riding ring; it should be the normal rhythm for cross-country hacking, because it is the least tiring form of canter.

In the *extended canter*, the lengthening of the horse's posture (moving the center of gravity forward) is even more pronounced than at the medium canter. As a result, the strides are longer and the horse requires firmer support. But it should never abandon its natural posture and lean on the rider's hands. When hunting, the speed of the canter averages four hundred to five hundred meters per minute (fifteen to eighteen miles per hour); on open terrain, it can be increased to the maximum (gallop), but this is only possible over relatively short distances, taking into consideration the ground conditions and the horse's natural ability. In the extended canter, the rider should follow the increased forward displacement of the horse's center of gravity by rising from the saddle and taking a half seat—in other words, the jumping seat when jumping, the hunting seat when hunting, and the racing seat when racing (Fig. 28).

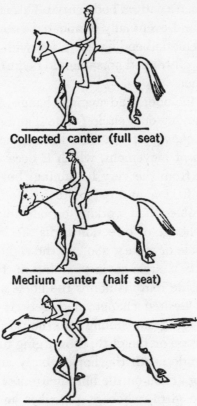

Collected canter (full seat)

Medium canter (half seat)

Gallop (racing seat)

FIG. 28. *The canter and the gallop.*

8. *Work on One Track*

Work on one track consists in keeping the horse perfectly straight, even when following a curved line (with the forehand and hindquarters moving on the same track). It enables the rider to acquire equestrian tact, to learn to use the aids and to combine them correctly, and thus to dominate his horse effectively; at the same time, it trains the horse to obey the rider's commands while producing gaits that are relaxed, supple, and in balance. The purpose of these exercises is to give the horse gymnastic training in bending itself laterally, always taking into account the one-sided stiffness caused by the animal's natural body curve. This natural asymmetry can be corrected and eventually eliminated entirely by means of frequent and systematic bending exercises, with emphasis on the defective side. A well-trained horse should be just as supple on one side as on the other.

These exercises include: 1. advancing change of direction (turning corners); 2. moving on a circle (volte); and 3. the serpentine.

The *advancing change of direction* has a practical purpose; to alter the direction of movement, which is occasionally necessary in the riding ring from the very beginning; but it is also an excellent exercise in flexion, and it should therefore be practiced as frequently as possible when working on one track.

An advancing change of direction turns the horse 90° or, as a half turn (half circle or volte), 180°, to the right or to the left. It can be performed in a circle having a radius of three, two, or only one stride. The inside rein maintains the horse's head in position and indicates the desired change of direction; the outside rein prevents the forehand from "falling into the turn." The inside leg exerts a driving action on the girth, thus urging the inside hind leg farther forward underneath the horse's body and, as necessary, exerts a restraining action on the hindquarters. The outside leg is placed behind the girth, where it provokes an inflexion of the hindquarters around the inside leg and prevents the outside hind leg from deviating to the outside. It is important for the horse, starting from a straight position, to produce a correct inflexion, then to follow exactly the arc of the circle, and finally to resume a straight position upon completion of the movement. Many horses attempt to slow down the rhythm as they turn, and this should never be permitted; any such tendency should immediately be combated by the driving action of the aids.

The flexion of the horse's body displaces the center of gravity sideways toward the inside. In order to remain seated in equilibrium, the rider must also shift his own center of gravity toward the inside and thus increase the load on his inside buttock. He does so by leaning the upper part of his body sideways, without, however, bending the inside hip or leaving the outside shoulder behind. The degree of inclination depends principally on the horse's flexion, but also partially on the speed of the movement (centrifugal force), and it must be determined by the rider's feeling. He should be warned, however, against any exaggeration in leaning sideways, which is the tendency of many horsemen. For if the rider's center of gravity is too radically shifted, his seat, and consequently the action of the aids, will suffer, and the horse's balance will be disturbed as well; as a result, the horse will defend itself against such a burden and in doing so it will become stiff and inflexible.

Turning a corner is merely an advancing change of direction and is therefore achieved by the same aid actions. If the horse attempts to round off the corner too much, the rider should guide it into the corner by means of the outside rein, reinforced by the action of the inside leg (Fig. 29).

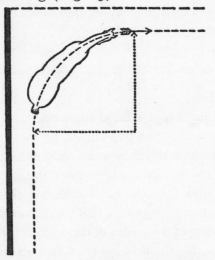

FIG. 29. *An advancing change of direction (turning a corner) turns the horse ninety degrees in a circle having a radius of three strides.*

Moving on a circle (volte) obliges the horse to bend itself inward laterally, the inside hind legs becoming more strongly flexed at the joints and engaged farther forward underneath the body. This tends to increase the animal's suppleness and consequently its ability to perform all the turns, the canter, and the lateral movements. The rider's actions are the same as during the advancing changes of direction, and his aids should be exactly adjusted

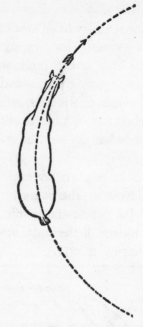

FIG. 30. *Moving on a circle.*

to the curve of the circle on which the horse is moving (Fig. 30).

A change of hand on the large circle can take place in the circle itself or, when working on two circles, by moving from one to the other. In both cases, the change is made on a line in the form of an S which, in the first case, passes through the center of the circle and, in the second, joins the two circles together. At each change the horse must take the position that corresponds to the new direction upon arriving at the center of the curve. If the rider is working at a rising trot, he should change diagonals at the same point. The change of leads at a canter should also take place in the center of the circle, unless the rider wishes to continue at the counter-canter.

The identical aids, suitably adapted, should be used on the small circle and in all other similar figures which are composed of half circles (serpentines, half turns) or quarter circles (advancing changes of direction, turning corners).

When *moving on a serpentine*, the rider must constantly modify the horse's position (flexion) and consequently the action of his aids, which are similar to those used when moving on a circle (during a change of hand); it is therefore a particularly worth-while training exercise for the rider as well as for the horse. It is most important to begin by displacing the weight to the new inside side and to modify the actions of the aids gradually, but still at the most opportune moment. At the rising trot, the rider must also change the diagonal correctly with each new position. The serpentine is particularly well suited for practicing the counter-canter.

However, work on one track should not be limited to circles and serpentines. All of the exercises that require the horse to produce flexion and to change its position frequently are extremely useful. The most varied figures can be performed; continual changes have an excellent educational effect and oblige both rider and horse to remain constantly alert. The most advantageous schooling for both of them is to spend the greatest part of their time on exercises of this kind, and to reserve the work on straight lines (especially on the outside track) almost exclusively for fast gaits.

9. *The Rein-back*

The *rein-back* (stepping backward) is of practical value, but above all it is an extremely profitable exercise for the rider and, at the same time, a means of testing the responsiveness of the horse and its ability to maintain its balance.

The rein-back is no more than a reinforced halt, as far as the action of the aids is concerned. If the rider, after having come to a full halt, continues to apply the same aids, he obliges the horse to step backward. The nature of the movement, in which the fore-legs rather than the hindquarter play the propulsive role, indicates that the aids should naturally act from front to back, that is to say, in the opposite direction of their action in producing forward movement. This action, which is in no way artificial, is immedi-ately and perfectly understood by a horse that is well in hand during movement as well as at a standstill.

However, before starting to practice the rein-back, the rider should already have acquired sufficient feeling for co-ordinating the aids so that he is able to maintain, during forward movement and at the halt, a refined and constant contact with the horse's mouth.

Once the horse has been brought to a halt correctly while remaining responsive to the rein aids, it can be urged to move backward by a supple action of the reins toward the rear; the rider's legs, placed in a normal position, guard against any incorrect placement of the hind legs. Throughout the movement, the small of the back should be supplely stretched and the upper part of the body held erect. A sufficient engagement of the hind legs under the animal's body is obtained by the halt that precedes the rein-back, and by the rein-back itself. In these conditions, the horse should back up step by step in a straight line. It should interrupt the movement immediately—that is, stop—the moment the rider ceases to ask it to back up, in other words, as soon as the appropriate action of the reins is discontinued and the rider's hands have become passive again. If, however, the horse continues to back, the rider should immediately prevent it from doing so by bringing into play the driving aids. If necessary, a touch of the spur will impress upon the horse that it must not repeat the fault the next time.

The alternating pulls on the reins which urge first the forelegs and then, diagonally, the hind legs to move backward make these rein actions very effective ones, and thus they provide valuable exercise for the development of the rider as well as for the horse.

For the purposes of training, and in order not to strain the joints of the hind legs, the rider need not ask for more than five or six backing steps at a time.

When the horse can perform the rein-back without resistance, calmly, keeping its head and neck in the same position and moving backward in a straight line step by step, and when the rider is able to stop it at any moment, or immediately move forward at any desired gait and rhythm, it is a difficult but undeniable proof of the horse's degree of schooling and of the rider's skill as a horseman.

10. *The Countercanter*

The *countercanter* (canter on the "wrong lead") is a canter to the
right intentionally performed on the left lead, or a canter to the
left on the right lead. However, it is a true countercanter only
when the horse is bent in the direction opposite to the normal
position (Fig. 31). Consequently, the difficulty of this gait resides

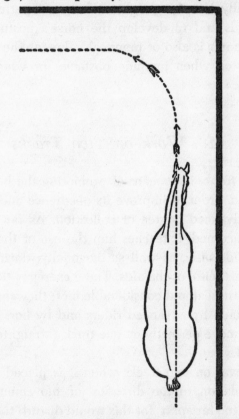

FIG. 31. *The horse's position for striking off into a countercanter to the left.*

in the contradiction existing between the canter position that must
be conserved and the lateral flexion that would normally correspond to the direction of the movement. This requires that the
rider take a correspondingly firmer seat and intensify the action

of the aids that maintain the horse in a correct canter position.

The countercanter should be performed only over very short distances at a reduced rhythm, and only by horses that are well balanced during forward movement. All the changes of direction made at this gait should, at the beginning, be executed on a wide curve; the rider must possess sufficient training and be sufficiently independent of his horse's movements to be able to prevent the animal from changing its lead by intensifying his aids. Schooling in the countercanter on a large circle or on a serpentine (with the turns eventually becoming tighter) helps to perfect the rider's use of the aids and to develop the horse's posture (balance). The countercanter is also of practical value, as the rider will appreciate later on when jumping obstacles or when riding over varied terrain.

11. *Work on Two Tracks*

Work on two tracks is a means of promoting the horse's physical development in order to improve its obedience and to prepare it for a more advanced degree of collection. As far as the rider's training is concerned, it teaches him the use of the rein and leg aids on one side only, as well as diagonally, during movement, and perfects his sense of the aids. These exercises demand as preconditions a firm seat and considerable tact; they should therefore be practiced only by advanced riders and by horses that are already able to move perfectly on one track (straightened) and are well balanced.

A horse moves on two tracks when it is placed in an oblique position in relation to the direction of movement. The tracks should not be too far apart, for this would disturb the even succession of hoofbeats. The forehand always precedes the hindquarters, while one lateral pair of legs crosses in front of the other pair.

The horse can move on two tracks at all gaits—that is, at the walk, trot, and canter—but only at slow speeds, due to its lateral position. It is most important for the gaits to be perfectly even

JUMPING   9. The take-off.

PHOTO: O. Cornaz, L'Année Hippique-Paddock, Lausanne

PHOTO: O. Cornaz, L'Année Hippique-Paddock, Lausanne

JUMPING   11. The landing.

JUMPING   12.   A broad jump.

and vigorous. All of these exercises should be performed only during very brief periods.

Depending upon the position of the horse and the kind of movement that results, there are: 1. leg yielding; and 2. side steps.

Leg yielding is a movement on two tracks which are only a half step apart, in which the inside lateral pair of legs crosses in front of the outside pair. The position of the horse's head adjusts itself to the rider's laterally driving leg, that is, it is turned opposite to the direction of movement (Fig. 32).

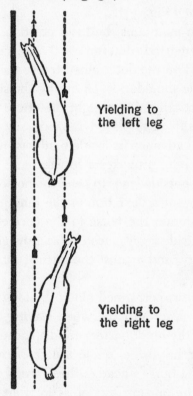

Yielding to
the left leg

Yielding to
the right leg

FIG. 32. *Leg yielding.*

The inside rein maintains the head in the correct position. The outside rein supports, in order to prevent any exaggerated flexion of the neck or a deviation of the outside shoulder.

The rider places his inside leg immediately behind the girth where it urges the horse to move sideways. His outside leg is placed against the girth and, by a restraining action, limits the action of the inside leg, at the same time urging the horse into the desired direction of movement.

The *side steps* require a higher degree of schooling in both horse and rider. They consist of: 1. the shoulder in; 2. the travers; and 3. the renvers.

In the *shoulder in,* the horse moves on two tracks that are one step apart, with the inside legs crossing in front of the outside legs. As in leg yielding, the horse's head is turned away from the direction of movement (Fig. 33).

The inside rein maintains the head position, while the outside rein, suitably supported, determines the degree of the position, directs the animal on the determined track, and prevents a deviation of the outside shoulder. Even during the side steps, the reins should always act only in a straight direction.

The rider's inside leg, placed immediately behind the girth, urges the horse to advance its inside hind leg and, in collaboration with the outside rein, provokes a forward and lateral movement. The action of the outside leg is to bend the horse's body around the inside leg, to prevent a deviation of the hindquarters, and at the same time to maintain the horse in the correct movement. Consequently, the outside leg is placed behind the girth if a restraining action is necessary, and against the girth if its aim is to promote impulsion.

The shoulder in is performed along the long wall of the riding ring and is most easily initiated when leaving the corner.

In the *travers,* the hindquarters are displaced by approximately one step toward the inside, while the forehand remains on the original track. The horse's head is thus turned in the direction of the movement; the outside legs cross in front of the inside legs (Fig. 33).

The inside rein guides the horse and at the same time maintains the correct head position and the appropriate flexion. The outside rein limits the degree of the horse's oblique position and prevents a deviation by the outside shoulder.

The inside leg, placed against the girth, maintains the advanc-

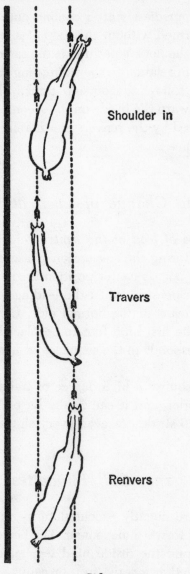

Shoulder in

Travers

Renvers

FIG. 33. *Side steps.*

ing movement by urging the inside hind leg forward. The outside leg, placed immediately behind the girth, maintains the horse's flexion and the lateral movement. The rider's seat should be inclined toward the direction of movement.

The travers is most easily performed along the long side wall of the riding ring, immediately after coming out of a corner; but it can also be performed without the help of a wall.

In the *renvers*, the horse's position is the same as in the travers, but it is reversed in relation to the riding-ring wall—that is to say, the hindquarters follow the outside track, while the forehand moves one step toward the inside on the second track (Fig. 33).

The aids required by the renvers are therefore just the same as for the travers.

12. *Flying Change of Lead at the Canter*

The flying change of lead at the canter (change of lead in the air) takes place during the suspension phase of the canter. The rider changes the horse's canter position at the moment previous to the phase of suspension, when the leading leg is still touching the ground, by means of the normal aids. Consequently, in the very next stride the first hind foot to be placed on the ground is the one that corresponds to the sequence of hoofbeats of the new canter.

This exercise requires a high degree of training on the part of both horse and rider, and it can finally be performed as desired every three or two strides, or even every single stride.

13. *Half Pirouettes*

Half pirouettes are fluently executed turns on the hindquarters performed during forward movement. The horse turns, describing a half circle, around the inside hind leg, maintaining whatever gait it was in, whether a walk, trot, or canter.

As in the turns on the hindquarters, the horse is urged to move around its inside hind leg by the action of the rider's outside leg in collaboration with the reins. The rider's inside leg does not restrain (does not limit) the movement, as is the case during the turn on the hindquarters, because the half pirouette is not performed step by step but in a supple, continuous manner. In this case, the principal task of the inside leg is to prevent the horse from backing.

The best preliminary exercise for the half pirouette (which should first be performed at a walk) is a turn on the hindquarters or a half turn (half circle or volte). In the first case, the rider tries to place the horse in a suitable position at the same time he brings it to a halt, and then immediately makes it take the first lateral step (at a walk, during the early lessons). During a half turn, on the other hand, the rider tries to make the turn tighter and tighter by means of the outside leg, and the entire movement should be performed in a continuous and supple manner.

The half pirouette requires of the horse an already high degree of collection, and of the rider a very precise and refined action of the aids. At the same time, it is only of limited practical value and therefore primarily constitutes (as do, for similar reasons, the flying change of lead at the canter and the work on two tracks) a preparation for and transition to high-school dressage, in which two successive half pirouettes, describing a complete circle, become the "pirouette."

CHAPTER 4

JUMPING

JUMPING

1. *The Horse During the Jump*

The jump made by a horse when clearing an obstacle scarcely differs from the springs it performs during the canter. The sequence of hoofbeats is based on exactly the same principle, but the obstacle separates the support of the forelegs from that of the hind legs. The flight phase therefore starts at the moment the hind legs leave the ground. A horse can jump from any gait and even from a standstill, but since the jump usually produces a canter position, the animal, after clearing the obstacle, in principle always moves on at a canter.

The propulsive force which enables the horse to jump normally comes from the strong thrust and sudden relaxation of the muscles of the hindquarters at the moment of the take-off, reinforced by the animal's acquired momentum, which varies according to the speed and gait at which the obstacle is met. These two forces complement and can replace each other up to a certain point and in a certain proportion, depending on the nature of the obstacle and the conformation of the horse.

A high, straight obstacle that requires a high but short jump should be approached on a shortened stride, permitting the horse to take off at an appropriate angle of ascent by means of a suitable flexion and by engaging its hind legs well underneath its body. In this case, it is the propulsive force of the hindquarters that plays the principal role. If, on the other hand, the obstacle is wide and low, the horse should approach it at a faster and more extended stride, so that the jump will also be low and long. In this instance, the horse's momentum reduces to a certain extent the amount of impulsion that must be provided by the hindquarters.

From this we can draw the following conclusions: The slower the pace at the moment the obstacle is met (or when jumping from a standstill), the greater is the work of the *hindquarters* and the less that of the forehand. But the faster the pace, the more the *forehand* participates in the effort by receiving all of the momentum acquired at the moment of the take-off and by giving this force a corresponding direction; moreover, at the moment of landing, it is the forehand that must support the kinetic energy of the entire mass and maintain it in equilibrium.

We know, for example, that a horse possessing sturdy, well-constructed hindquarters, but whose shoulders are very straight or whose forelegs are weak, can jump rather high obstacles at a slow pace. However, as a general rule, the same horse is apt to jump badly when driven toward the obstacle at a faster speed, or toward an obstacle that is very broad. Conversely, a horse possessing a good forehand but weak and badly articulated hindquarters is able to jump at a fast pace over rather broad obstacles, while he will most often jump badly over high ones and those that are approached at a slow speed—in other words, when a great muscular effort of the hindquarters is required.

Consequently, as far as conformation is concerned, the best jumpers are horses possessing well-muscled hindquarters, well-articulated hind legs, a strong back, long sloping shoulders, a long neck, and not too small a head. The *hindquarters determine the propulsive force and the forehand determines the speed at which a horse jumps best. The role of the neck and head is to determine how these two fundamental elements of the jump are combined, to regulate their action, and to enable them to function in harmony.*

According to whether the angle in which the propulsive force of the hindquarters acts is more or less acute, the result is a long jump or a high jump. The distance a horse is capable of jumping exceeds only relatively slightly the distance it spans during one stride of the canter. On the other hand, its capacity for high jumping depends on special aptitudes and training. Under favorable conditions, a horse can clear an obstacle well over seven feet high.

The horse's physical conformation determines the pace at which it jumps the best. It adapts this pace to the nature of the obstacle and, when mounted, to the rider's weight as well.

The jump itself is composed of a series of different kinds of movements, each of which necessitates a different posture on the part of the horse. We can distinguish three principal phases during the jump: the take-off, the flight phase, and the landing.

During the *take-off*, the horse engages its hind legs suitably far underneath the body, raises its forehand off the ground by the thrust of the forelegs and by elevating its head; it is then projected into the air by the sudden contraction and release of the hind leg joints and of the back, and by stretching forward its neck and head.

During the *flight phase*, in the course of which the obstacle is cleared, the horse describes an arc (a parabola), keeping its back relaxed (bascule), its neck outstretched, and its legs folded. This phase can be divided into two sections: the ascent to the highest point of the parabola, and the descent down to the landing.

Upon *landing*, the horse stretches out its forelegs and successively places both forefeet on the ground, decreasing the burden on the forelegs by an appropriate raising of the head and neck. Then it extends the hind legs and places them behind the forelegs, lowers the head in order to resume its normal carriage, and resumes its forward movement at a canter.

In the course of these different movements that make up a jump, the horse's posture is modified several times in quick succession, thus displacing its center of gravity, and it is particularly important for the rider to understand these changes if he is to remain constantly seated in equilibrium (Fig. 34).

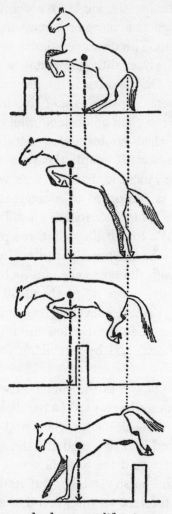

FIG. 34. *During the jump the horse modifies its posture several times and thus also alters the location of its center of gravity.*

2.   *The Rider During the Jump*

From the rider's point of view, there are two other phases of the jump in addition to the three we have just described: the moments immediately before and immediately following the jump. Consequently, the rider's comportment during the jump consists of five phases: 1. the approach to the obstacle; 2. the take-off; 3. the flight phase; 4. the landing; 5. continuing the forward movement.

During the *approach* to the obstacle, the important thing is to present the horse in front of the obstacle at a well regulated pace and in a straight direction.

A jump is normally made from the canter or gallop, because this is the easiest jumping gait for the rider as well as for the horse. But for schooling purposes the jump can also be performed at a trot and even a walk if the obstacles are not too high. In jumps of this kind the momentum is very limited, and the animal is obliged to furnish a greater muscular effort. On the other hand, the rider, who is not pulled along by the movement but who still has to follow the horse as it extends itself at the take-off, is given practice in maintaining a firmer and more sensitive seat. At all gaits, the rhythm should be lively but at the same time regular and calm. It should be neither listless nor too fiery and impetuous, neither slowing down when nearing the obstacle nor speeding up. Such alterations of pace can only result in complicating the jumping process or even in rendering it impossible. The spirit of judicious determination in the approach is decisive at the jump itself.

The rider's seat depends on the particular gait and cadence that exist at the moment the obstacle is met. Across country, as well as in the jumping ring (over a jumping course), the rider usually has to jump at least from a strong canter and most often from a gallop. Therefore when the rider arrives at the obstacle, he should be in a half seat with a sufficient forward inclination (jumping seat). With the knees and heels well down, the legs are placed flat and firmly at the rear edge of the girth, where they can effect a driving action, and they should remain in this position throughout the entire jump. The feet are placed in the stirrups so that their widest part is on the front edge of the stirrup irons (Fig. 35). If they were pushed all the way "home," it would cause the feet and knees to be raised, and the legs to loosen their grip, so that in most cases they would slip toward the rear, and the entire seat, as well as the action of the aids, would be affected.

If the rider has to restrain the horse because it leans too heavily

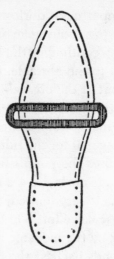

FIG. 35. *The foot is placed in the stirrup so that the widest part is on the front edge of the stirrup iron.*

on the reins (active weight aids), or if the horse slows down or "props" when approaching an obstacle, the rider must take a fuller seat in order not to be pushed in front of the horse's center of gravity (passive weight aids); otherwise, he could not effectively urge the horse forward, and the elevation of the forehand—and consequently the jump itself—would become impossible.

Only experienced riders can permit themselves, for schooling purposes, to approach an obstacle obliquely or when coming out of a turn, in other words, to jump out of a curve. As a general rule, the rider should direct the horse by the normal action of the aids to a take-off position perpendicular to the obstacle and at its center.

The *take-off* can be influenced to a certain extent by the gait and cadence of the approach; but if the rider tries to *impose* upon the horse the moment or the type of take-off, his intervention would be not only useless but extremely harmful. He should behave as passively as possible from the moment of the take-off until the landing, and he should adjust his seat as well as his aids, particularly the rein and weight aids, in order to give his horse the greatest possible freedom and to facilitate its maintenance of equilibrium. Only in this way can the rider remain in equilibrium at the take-off and during the rest of the jump, and thus preserve the horse's balance, which is only too easily disturbed.

The rider should take a forward-inclined half seat (jumping seat) adapted to the elevation of the horse's forehand and its ensuing extension. His hands should follow the horse's extending head and neck while maintaining a passive contact with the mouth. Without this free extension of its head and neck (forward displacement of the center of gravity), the horse would be even more handicapped in jumping than a man would be if his arms were tied behind his back.

This adjustment of the rider's seat should not be very difficult if the jump is executed in a fluent fashion, at a rapid pace, and if the rider is already correctly seated because he is following the movement—in other words, if the seat is dictated by the pace. However, the situation is entirely different when the jump takes place from a slow pace or from a standstill. In these cases, the rider must take care not to miss the most favorable moment for the take-off. If he leans forward prematurely, he can lose his balance to the front, with the result that the forehand will be overburdened at the moment of elevation—perhaps making the take-off impossible or even leading to the rider's falling off over the horse's head. If, on the other hand, the rider leans forward too late—as is more frequently the case—he loses his balance to the rear, that is to say, he remains behind the horse's movement, overburdening the hindquarters and thus reducing the propulsive force of the take-off (Fig. 36).

The flight phase commences as soon as the horse has left the ground.

During the *flight phase*, the rider should remain absolutely passive in a forward-inclined half seat (jumping seat) and should take care to place himself on the longitudinal axis of the horse's body so that he will not spoil the animal's lateral balance by leaning to the side. His hands, following the horse's mouth forward, should maintain a light contact by means of the reins.

While this support by the reins is an essential point in all equitation, in this instance it is particularly necessary if the forward movement is to be resumed smoothly immediately after the landing. However, whenever the rider can no longer follow the horse's extension with his seat, it is better to abandon all support by the reins rather than to render impossible the requisite extension of the neck, head, and back during the jump, by hanging onto the reins and pulling the horse back. In this case, or when the rider's hands are stretched as far forward as possible but still cannot follow the mouth, the rider should allow the necessary additional portion of rein to slide through his fingers.

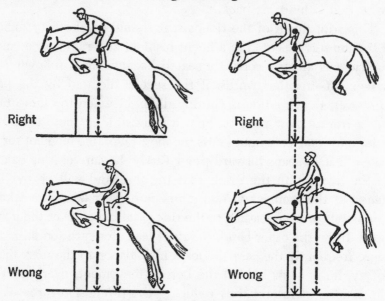

Right   Right

Wrong   Wrong

FIG. 36. *The rider's seat during the take-off.*
FIG. 37. *The rider's seat during the flight phase.*

The rider should not rest his hands and reins on the horse's mane, for they would lose not only their freedom of action but also their suppleness and sensitivity. During the jump, the hands should be completely independent of the seat; their correct position, determined by the placement of the horse's mouth, is on each side of the animal's neck (Fig. 37).

During the *landing*, in order not to disturb the horse's balance, the rider must adapt his seat, not only to the horse's posture, but also to the angle of descent, which depends upon the type of obstacle being jumped. The steeper the inclination of the horse's back, the less forward-inclined should be the rider's seat, until finally, during very steep landings (which occur only rarely) the rider's seat will be completely vertical. With his knees acting as springs, he absorbs the shock caused by the landing and resumes his normal half seat as soon as the horse's hind feet have touched the ground (Figs. 38 and 39).

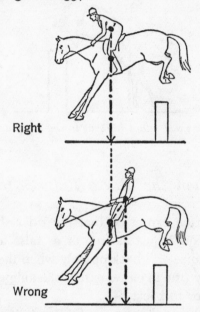

Right

Wrong

FIG. 38. *The rider's seat during the landing.*

The horse utilizes the support of the reins as soon as its feet are once more on the ground. If it has lost this support during the course of the jump, the rider should re-establish it as supply but also as rapidly as possible, although in many cases—for example, when the horse stumbles—this is easier said than done.

Continuing the forward movement, the rider immediately places his horse on the aids again so that he will be able to influence the animal as circumstances may require.

If another jump follows, the horse is brought into the rhythm that is appropriate for the following obstacle, and directed toward it in a straight line.

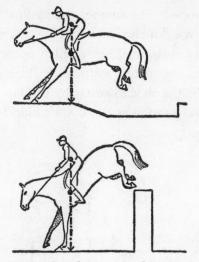

FIG. 39. *The rider must adapt his seat to the steepness of the landing.*

3. When the Horse Refuses to Jump

The opinion is often expressed that the rider should "force" his horse to jump. This is just as true or as false as saying, for example, that the horse will back up only when the rider "forces" it to do so. It is only true in either case if the animal has never been *trained* to jump or to back.

A well-trained horse that has confidence in its rider will always obey him and will jump well and willingly according to its ability. The only horses who stop or run out are those that lack confidence in their rider—and it so happens that they lose this confidence more easily in jumping than in any other field of equitation. Most often, especially with very sensitive animals, it requires no more than a moment's inattention, a simple oversight, a jerk of the mouth, a jolt on the back, a jab of the spur, or an inopportune use of the whip, an obstacle incorrectly set up, or something of the kind. Afterward it may take months of patient work to re-establish the confident relationship that is essential between the horse and rider, and even then the distrust may not disappear entirely.

Jumping should be a part of every horse's training. However, only an animal that is perfectly placed on the aids and physically well trained can become a good jumper and be successfully ridden over difficult obstacles. This admittedly requires specialized training and practice.

When a trained horse runs out or stops in front of a jump, it is certainly not simple disobedience; there is some reason that has made it impossible to jump. A horse is not a machine; it can be ailing or sick, it can stumble or slip, it can misjudge the obstacle or the correct moment for the take-off, and there may be many other reasons, which the experienced rider will understand and take into account, according to the particular circumstances.

If a horse refuses to jump because of stubbornness, it should be punished as a matter of training, though in 99 per cent of the cases it is probably due to an error by the rider, either at the moment of the jump or even earlier during the preparation. In no case should the punishment be an expression of anger; it should help the rider to overcome the horse's resistance in the most effective and most reasonable manner.

A horse can fail to jump either by refusing (stopping) or by running out.

In *refusing*, it stops short in front of the obstacle. In order to do so, it must either gradually slow down the rhythm, or else come to a very abrupt stop. If it slows down, the driving aids should intervene promptly and prevent the reduction of speed, thereby preventing the refusal. An experienced rider can usually sense his horse's intention to stop suddenly in front of an obstacle, and he can often combat it successfully by an appropriate driving action of the aids.

Nevertheless, if the horse *has* refused, and if the jump cannot be made from a standstill, either the horse must be backed up directly away from the obstacle, or else, after retreating a few steps, then turned sharply, and ridden energetically back to the obstacle.

In *running out*, the horse turns away from the obstacle of its own initiative, to the right or to the left, in order to avoid jumping.

It usually increases the pace because it wishes, so to speak, to "run away from" the obstacle.

The rider often can prevent this evasion if he reacts in time. For example, if the horse wishes to run out to the left (which is usually its most flexible side), the rider can prevent it from doing so by suitable restraining actions of the reins. At the same time, he should make the horse turn on its axis by acting with the right rein and the right leg, placed behind the girth, in order to keep the horse headed straight toward the obstacle. On the other hand, it would be a mistake in this case to use the right rein and the *left* leg in order to bend or move the horse diagonally to the right. In general, a horse that tends to run out will not obey such an action of the aids.

If, in spite of these efforts, the horse succeeds in running out, the rider should ride it back to the obstacle by circling in the opposite direction to the direction of the evasion. He should protect himself from a recurrence of the incident by supporting with the corresponding rein and by restraining with the leg on the same side.

After a disobedience by stopping or running out, the horse should always be made to jump. In no case should it be put back in the stable feeling that it has won. However, it is only sensible, in certain circumstances, first to lower the obstacle in question, and thus content oneself—at least for the moment—with only a half victory.

4. *Training the Rider to Jump*

The rider should have acquired a certain security in the saddle before beginning to jump, and also learned to influence the horse to a certain degree. In any case, he should have at least several hours of schooling at the canter to his credit.

At the very beginning and as a preliminary preparation to actual jumping, he can be asked to ride over a few poles placed on the ground, first at a walk and then at a trot. The rider should use a posting trot, and it is advantageous to have him touch the base of the horse's neck with his right or left hand at the moment when the horse steps over the poles. Very soon the poles may be raised to a height of eighteen inches to two feet, placing them in such a way that the horse is unable to run out (against the wall of the indoor ring, or with wings on either side).

It is best to begin by jumping only at a canter, because it is easiest and most agreeable at this gait for the rider as well as for the horse. No rein actions should be used during this training over fences until the rider's hands have acquired enough independence from his seat to enable him to avoid disturbing the horse with the reins during the jump. Until he possesses a sufficient sense of equilibrium when jumping, the rider may hold onto the mane, but never the pommel, which would considerably handicap him in following the horse's movement with his seat, and he must try to do so from the very start. A correct jumping seat, which always implies an appropriate distribution of weight, should never be neglected in favor of relatively minor details. The most important points to seek are a straight back (in no case hunched over), knees held low and flat, sensitive legs clinging closely to the girth, and low heels. The rider's gaze should be directed straight ahead and beyond the obstacle.

As soon as the rider can jump without holding onto the mane, he can be asked to reach out during the jump with his hands (which are now independent of his seat), moving them forward on each side of the horse's neck toward its mouth. Certain other exercises, like the "hands on the hips" or the "crossed arms," make it considerably more difficult to follow the horse's movement, and it is better to ignore them. It is also disadvantageous to have the rider raise his arms or stretch them sideways during a jump, since these exercises may have a harmful effect on the subsequent action of the reins.

At this stage, the rider can begin jumping from a posting trot, a gait that improves the seat and develops the sensitive feeling which enables the rider to adapt himself to the horse's movement. As soon as he performs these exercises without any special difficulty, he can start to hold the reins.

At the beginning, the novice jumper should school only over a single jump, then over two, three, and four (the maximum), following in close succession. The separating distances should be of eight paces (twenty-four feet) for a normal canter (ordinary canter), and only seven paces (twenty-one feet) for a trot (ordinary trot). If later on the jump is to be taken from a more extended canter, the distance between the obstacles should be increased even more.* These distances are calculated so that the horse must make one stride between each obstacle in order to be well placed for the take-off at the following one. The rhythmical repetition of successive jumps (in and out) is particularly helpful in developing the jumping technique of the rider.

These exercises are even more beneficial if the type and appearance of the last obstacle of the series is varied in order to familiarize the rider with the different obstacles, singly and in combination. When the rider is sufficiently advanced so that he no longer interferes with the horse with his seat (equilibrium) or hands, a complete jumping course can be set up with a variety of different obstacles, in order to teach him to regulate the horse ever more surely and intelligently.

It is also often necessary to take into account certain psychological factors during the rider's jumping training. It is important that jumping should not be considered a special event. Everything should take place during the normal schooling session, the lessons succeeding one another in a logical and natural sequence. Not only should the rider lose any fear of falling, but he should take an increased interest and pleasure in jumping. For this, he needs not only intelligence, but determination as well. The rider must learn to jump also with his head and his heart!

---

* It is not the gait as such, but rather the pace at which the obstacle will be approached (take-off speed) that determines the spacing for obstacles placed in combination. That is why the tempo of the gait must be kept steady even at the expense of its correctness.

CHAPTER 5

IN THE OPEN COUNTRY

IN THE OPEN COUNTRY

13. LEFT, On forest trails.

14. BELOW, Crossing a stream.

IN THE OPEN COUNTRY   15. Riding uphill.

PHOTO: O. Cornaz, *L'Année Hippique-Paddock*, Lausanne

16. Jumping into water.

IN THE OPEN COUNTRY

17. Jumping on a bank.

PHOTO: Jean Bridel, *L'Année Hippique*, Lausanne

IN THE OPEN COUNTRY   18. Riding downhill.

IN THE OPEN COUNTRY

1. *Riding over Roads and across Country*

As soon as the rider has acquired sufficient security in the saddle to be able to guide his horse, he can begin schooling in the open country over varied terrain. This training is extremely important, for it is the most natural way of developing a supple seat and of making the rider independent. In the open country, his behavior toward his horse should be exclusively aimed at achieving the immediate goal, and it should be adapted to the goal in question. This adaptation to a particular goal trains the rider better and more rapidly than all the more or less regimented methods. In riding over varied terrain, the rider and his mount bring into evidence their abilities and skill, while weaknesses that were not apparent in the riding ring will be clearly exposed.

In the open country, you can ride alone or in a group with other riders. A *group* in this case is an unorganized formation of riders led by the instructor, who rides three horses' lengths ahead of the others. When going out with a group, each rider should maintain as far as possible the place he originally took in relation to his companions during the entire ride; in any case, he should not overtake or cut in front of or across the other riders. The instructor guides the group by voice or, better still, by gesture, but especially by setting an example of the gait and rhythm and by leading the group in the desired direction. Particular care should be taken to see that all the riders maintain a calm and regular rhythm.

A ride in the open country is first of all an end in itself, as it constitutes the main object of the rider's training in the school gaits and in jumping. The rider should be able to cover a determined distance rapidly and without squandering his horse's strength, in other words, as economically as possible. This itinerary can follow more or less easy roads, or it can go across country over a terrain bristling with difficulties and obstacles.

Over roads, the problem consists primarily in apportioning and regulating the kinds of gaits and their rhythms according to the time in which the distance must be covered. You can move at a walk, trot, or canter, but always at a rhythm that is calculated to expend the horse's strength as rationally as possible, especially when the distance to be covered is a long one. In such a case, you should use a calm and regular rhythm, "marching rhythm," steadily maintained without variation, particularly at the trot, and which may be accelerated to a canter only over short distances.

Obliging the riders to stay at a very definite tempo enables them to develop a feeling of the speed at which they are moving at every moment; this feeling can also be further promoted by occasionally having them cover a measured distance at different gaits and tempos, verifying the time taken to cover the distance by means of a stop watch.

In order to cover one mile, it takes the horse sixteen minutes at an ordinary walk, eight minutes at an ordinary trot, and five minutes at a medium canter. Consequently, the rider covers almost four miles per hour at a walk. If he trots for ten minutes during this hour, he can cover almost four and a half miles per hour. By alternating ten minutes of walking and five minutes of trotting, he attains a speed of almost five miles per hour; by alternating ten minutes of trotting and ten minutes of walking he reaches a speed of five and a half miles per hour; and by alternating five minutes of walking and ten minutes of trotting, the speed will be almost six and a quarter miles per hour.

If a faster rate of march is desired, it is advisable to canter part of the time. For example, in the last case, if ten minutes of trotting is replaced by cantering, a speed of about seven miles per hour is obtained; if two ten-minute trotting periods are replaced by cantering, the speed will reach seven and a half miles per hour. In this way, very fit horses can canter as much as thirty minutes out of every hour, trotting or walking the rest of the time, and they can thus average a speed of eight to eight and a half miles per hour.

A good hunter is expected to cover a distance of a little over six miles in thirty minutes of cantering without a break, that is, at a speed of twelve and a half miles per hour. A good race horse covers five-eighths of a mile in about a minute, that is, at a speed of thirty-seven miles per hour.

Each ride should begin with about ten minutes of walking and end in the same way. On long rides, a ten- or fifteen-minute rest period must be given every two hours, during which the girth should be loosened and the saddle and bridle checked. In a "forced march" (a long-distance ride), the horse's speed is calculated so as to cover the first half of the distance in a longer time, therefore at a slower speed, than the second half. Speed affects most of all the heart and lungs, especially if a burst of speed is unusually prolonged, and it is therefore much more tiring to the horse; thus sustained speed is a matter of training, and its duration should be increased only gradually.

Riding across country can be complicated by various difficulties of terrain and of different types of obstacles. The rider must therefore have, not only an excellent knowledge of the equestrian art, but also a good eye for judging the nature and characteristics of the ground. He should choose the best path to follow well ahead, and he should reach his goal after expending the least possible amount of strength and time.

Clearing such obstacles as *hedges, walls, banks, fences,* etc., which often conceal the landing on the far side, requires a great deal of ingenuity, attentiveness, and prudence—qualities which should never degenerate into irresolution. The rider should take his bearings from as far away as possible, decide how and where he will approach the obstacle, and move toward it resolutely.

When going through a *woods,* it is necessary to respond very quickly in order to avoid the trees, by skillful turns (weight aids), without jerking on the reins.

Ditches that are dry and not too wide are approached and jumped from an accelerating pace. If they are very wide and dry, it may be advantageous first to jump down into them. This requires care if the ditch is filled with water, for the banks may be slippery with mud.

The rider should avoid as far as possible riding over very *marshy* terrain and *icy ground.* But if they cannot be circumvented, he must proceed at a quiet walk and permit the horse to maintain its balance more easily by leaning his body forward (unburdening the hindquarters) and by offering greater freedom from the reins. If the horse sinks in too deeply or slips, the rider must dismount and lead it by the reins, held long.

In the water, the rider must advance very cautiously at a walk, feeling his way on the ground. The greatest caution is necessary when the water is not clear, and he must always be prepared to encounter uneven depths. When crossing through running water with a rather strong current, the rider should place the horse in a slightly oblique position, opposite to the direction of the current. If his horse loses ground temporarily, he must release the stirrups, stretch his legs backward, and lean the upper part of his body on the horse's neck, grasping the mane with both hands. Under no circumstances should the reins interfere with the freedom of the horse's head and neck. If the horse is obliged to swim, the rider must let himself slide off its back to the left (always against the current, if it is strong) and allow himself to be pulled along in the water by holding onto the horse's mane.

When swimming in the water, horses sometimes try to turn around and swim back, or otherwise to stray from the proper direction; the rider should be able to correct these movements by means of light pulls on the appropriate rein.

When *riding uphill* in order to climb short, steep slopes, it is wise to gather momentum during the approach. On long slopes, however, it is better to adopt a slow speed, which saves the horse's strength. It is sometimes best to climb rather long and not very steep slopes on an oblique line.

The horse's movements when riding uphill are very similar to the movements of the jump during the take-off and the first part of the flight phase. The animal climbs a steep hill by making, so to speak, a series of little take-offs which require a great expenditure of energy by the hindquarters, the back, the neck, and the head. Generally speaking, the horse's posture is considerably extended.

Consequently, the rider must take a very forward-inclined half seat and give the horse complete freedom of its head. As it is not easy to maintain this seat, due to the steep slope of the horse's body and to the lack of speed, the rider should brace himself on the stirrups and also lean forward on the horse's neck and hold onto the mane (Fig. 40).

When *riding downhill,* the rider must constantly guide the horse in a straight line down the hill, since an oblique position can easily make it lose its balance (because its legs are not well adapted to a lateral support of the body), leading in many cases to the fall of both horse and rider.

The horse's movements when riding downhill are also very similar to those of the jump, during the last part of the phase in the air and at the landing. In order to displace its center of gravity to the rear, as the descent requires, the horse raises its head and neck and places its forefeet in front of each other, one by one. The position of the hindquarters is also similar to their position when landing after a jump, at the moment when the forefeet have already touched the ground and the hindquarters are still in the air. Consequently, the hindquarters play only a minor role when riding down a steep hill; they merely follow the forehand without being able to provide much support.

As a result, when riding downhill the rider should adapt his forward-inclined seat to the horse's posture and to its position resulting from the incline of the slope (and thus to its balance) just as he does when landing after a jump. The more sloping the line of the horse's back, the less the rider should incline his body for-

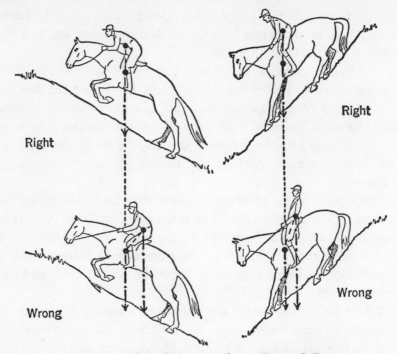

FIG. 40. *The rider's seat when riding uphill.*
FIG. 41. *The rider's seat when riding downhill.*

ward, so that on unusually steep slopes, which are ridden down (slid down) only exceptionally and only for very short distances, the rider's seat may even be vertical.

It goes without saying that this seat is very difficult to maintain, because such a body position, especially in the absence of speed, does not correspond to the rider's feeling for his own balance, which would require him to align himself with the vertical.* Consequently, in order to be able to maintain himself in such an insecure seat, the rider should seek a solid support, not only by gripping with his knees and by pressing on the stirrups, but sometimes by supporting his hands on the crest of the horse's neck as well (Figs. 41 and 42).

* The rider should not permit himself to be misled by this feeling. An inclination behind the horse's weight vector is a greater mistake than an inclination in front of the weight vector, because the overburdening of the horse's hind legs, which offer much less support in this instance, imperils the horse's efforts to maintain its balance.

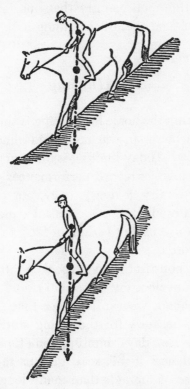

FIG. 42. *The rider must adapt his seat to the incline of the slope.*

The *rider's seat* when riding in the open country should always be adapted to both the posture and the momentary position of the horse. A shortened posture requires a full seat, when the animal's back is horizontal; any extension or inclination of the back, on the other hand, requires a forward-inclined half seat (jumping or hunting seat), but the rider should also take into consideration every lateral modification in the horse's posture and position.

Since its posture and position when riding over extremely varied terrain are constantly being modified, often with considerable rapidity, the rider should possess a very sensitive and supple seat in order to be always seated in equilibrium. He will also need great presence of mind and a swift grasp of every situation. It is therefore the best possible schooling and test for the rider as well as for the horse, since both of them are able to bring into play all of their abilities; and it is also the highest goal of practical riding.

It is in riding in the open country that one finds the heart and spirit, the alpha and omega, of the riding art.

2. *Hunting*

The origin of utilizing the horse for hunting is surely to be found in the distant times when man was nourished almost exclusively by the animals he killed. Today hunting is, of course, merely a sport, but as it does not involve record performances and consequently engenders neither rivalry, jealousy, envy, nor personal ambition, it should be considered the most classical equestrian sport. The special fascination of hunting is due, in fact, to the purely sporting pleasure it affords.

Hunting already constitutes, so to speak, a rather special field of equitation, which develops out of normal riding in the open country; on the other hand, we can consider that its goal is not exclusively sporting, because, for the riding student, it is also the best of schools. A few days' hunting sometimes develops more security and suppleness in his seat, greater tact, and more decisiveness in his use of the aids than many long and tiring hours of work in the riding ring.

Hunting on horseback can take place with or without hounds. When hounds are used, they may be coursing hounds or tracking hounds.

With coursing hounds, the quarry is always a living animal. These hounds, in fact, hunt by sight and not by scent and therefore they must always be able to see the game that they pursue. The game in this case is most often a hare or a fox. Driven from cover by the riders, it is pursued by one or two "unleashed" hounds. The riders follow them and the exciting hunt hurtles toward its unknown destination at a rapid speed. It comes to an end either at the "kill," when one of the hounds has seized the quarry by the neck, or else when the quarry succeeds in evading the sight of its pursuers and thus escapes.

This kind of hunting, the most splendid of all, requires a vast open terrain and therefore takes place today only in certain parts of Europe. For the riders, there hardly exists any greater and purer thrill than riding to the hunt behind coursing hounds.

The various breeds of tracking hounds use their sense of smell in order to pursue the game; a larger number is grouped in a "pack." The principal game is stag, wild boar, or again the fox. The hunt begins when the hounds pick up the scent, and ends at the kill, when the quarry, surrounded by the pack, receives the *coup de grâce*. The speed when hunting with a pack, in which the hounds must keep their noses on the trail of the game, is slower than when riding behind coursing hounds. In stag hunting, however, the riders are often obliged to make truly daring jumps. England is the traditional home of hunting with a pack of hounds.

In a "drag hunt," the live quarry is replaced by an artificial trail that is laid out by a rider who drags along at the end of a rope a bag or basket containing the "scent" (usually the excrement) of the fox. The hounds then follow this trail.

In a "paper chase," the quarry and dogs are replaced by bits of paper strewn along to mark a trail.

Sometimes the role of the quarry is played by a rider carrying a fox's brush (tail). In this case, the riders first gather at an appointed spot from where they can see the "quarry," and the real pursuit then starts. The brush must be removed from the rider's shoulder; it is the goal and prize of the hunt.

During the course of his first few hunts of whatever variety, the young rider is sure to run into all sorts of difficulties. Everything happens so quickly that he hardly has time to think. His actions and decisions, which must often be instantaneous, courageous, and even daring, should, however, never lead him astray from a correct and prudent behavior. Hunting with a pack of hounds requires, in addition to great presence of mind, a perfection that is acquired only by experience, thus with time.

First, it is necessary to have a suitable horse that can not only canter calmly and jump safely but is also perfectly placed on the aids. This is all the more important since the horses must move almost constantly at an extended canter or gallop and the riders must therefore be almost constantly in a half seat (hunting seat).

Even when all the horses are more or less carried away by the speed of the hunt, and thus move with greater animation, nothing is so disagreeable as to have a horse that constantly leans on the bit. Hunting should not become a struggle between the rider and his horse, or it would be neither pleasant nor worth while for either of them.

The rider should stay in his place in the "field," that is to say, his position in relation to the other members of the hunt, and he should follow his own path without pushing, passing, or crossing in front of his neighbors. If the field is led by a "master," the riders follow about fifty yards behind. In order to have a clear view, a rider must not follow exactly on the heels of the one preceding him, and even less jump in his tracks. The obstacles should be approached and jumped as straight as possible; an oblique jump can lead to a collision with a second rider and be extremely dangerous for both of them. The rider should also take care not to jump an obstacle side by side of a horse that is half a length ahead of him; his own mount, inspired by the example of the preceding horse, may jump at the same time, that is to say, half a length too soon, and this can have disastrous consequences, especially when the obstacle is widespread.

If a horse refuses in front of an obstacle, the rider should take care when attempting to retake the obstacle not to get in the way of, and so endanger, his companions. If the rider loses control of his horse, he should try to turn the horse to the side and then in a circle in order to bring it to hand again.

In no other field of riding can one discover the true character of a horse as well as when riding over varied terrain. It is only in God's open country that one can really learn what a horse is capable of, and exactly what is its true vocation.

CHAPTER 6

CONTINUING TO LEARN

CONTINUING TO LEARN

Even after the principles of the art of equitation in the ring, on the jumping course, and across country have been assimilated both in practice and in theory, if the rider imagines that there is nothing left to learn in any field of riding, he is making a serious mistake.

1. *Training Green Horses*

Nobody can really consider himself a complete horseman if he is unable to pass on his knowledge to young horses, that is, to train green horses. To be a horseman means above all being able to train horses.

It is a rich satisfaction to transform, all on one's own, a completely ignorant animal into a perfectly schooled and supple riding horse. It is also an extremely instructive activity, requiring a great deal of feeling, much technical knowledge, and above all a sharp insight into the psychology of the horse. And so a good horseman must be at the same time a good psychologist. Only then can he instill his horse with the necessary confidence and obtain the necessary obedience. He must know exactly when and how long he must behave gently and patiently toward his horse, and when, on the contrary, he must act with determination and authority in order to establish as rapidly as possible a complete and effective understanding and bend the animal to his will.

In training a green horse, the rider follows exactly the same series of exercises that he followed during his own training, taking care, however, to adapt them to the physical possibilities and

above all to the psychology of the individual animal. It is principally because of this psychological element that the rider, while
developing an ever-increasing degree of skill, can never attain
absolute perfection. Each horse poses new problems which the
rider can solve more or less successfully, according to his ability
and experience, but which always teach him something new. So
there always remains an infinite amount to learn!

2. *Versatility and Specialization*

Schooling in the riding ring, on the jumping course, and across
country are all parts of a whole. An all-purpose riding horse
should be equally well trained in all three fields and show proof
of the greatest possible versatility.

Each of these different phases of the art of riding can become,
of course, an object of specialization. Schooling in the riding ring,
when it is practiced consistently and developed, leads to high-
school dressage; training over fences leads to competitive show
jumping; riding across country leads to hunting; and training for
speed leads to steeplechase racing.

All-round schooling has various kinds of practical riding as a
goal, and its basic principle is therefore to give the horse as wide a
range of equilibrium as possible. The more differently, rapidly,
and accurately it is able to adapt its posture (balance) to the burden it carries, to the type of movement, and to the nature of the
ground, the more advanced its training as an all-purpose horse
can be considered to be. Such an animal should be able to adopt
the most suitable balance for all ordinary gaits as well as for clearing normal obstacles and overcoming the commonest difficulties
of open terrain.

High-school dressage is aimed at obtaining the highest degree
of collection in the horse's posture. Its goal is to acquire complete
control at shortened gaits and in movements in place which require a maximum shortening of the horse.

This art originated in the Middle Ages, in the days of steel-
sheathed knights who could not hope to obtain much speed from
their clumsy and often heavily armored steeds, and who therefore
needed to exercise the most perfect control over their horses. The

technique of battle during this period required a horse that could perform appropriate movements in a very limited space and even in place.

The art of dressage was developed to a very high degree first in Spain and later in Italy and France. But when it threatened to decline with the disappearance of chivalry, Emperor Charles VI founded in 1729 in Vienna the Spanish Court Riding School, based on the Spanish traditions, and there high-school dressage has been conserved in its purest form to this very day.

High-school dressage is divided into "the airs on the ground" and the "airs above the ground." To the former belong the *pirouette*, the *passage*, and the *piaffer;* to the latter the *levade*, the *courbette*, the *croupade*, the *ballotade*, and the *capriole.*

Jumping, as practiced in horse-show competitions, is the youngest branch of the riding arts. Its development has been possible only since the first decade of the present century, thanks to the jumping seat (half seat) which we owe to the Italian Captain Caprilli. Before him, the tradition was for jumping riders to lean their bodies backward.

With the introduction of this new seat, which is far better adapted to the horse's balance, jumping made great progress and the specialized training of horses and riders has led to a whole series of record performances.

Racing, which has been practiced since the most ancient times in a primitive way, assumed its present form in England during the last century. At the beginning, it was no more than a method of selecting superior horses for breeding, but it was later transformed into a sport, particularly after steeplechasing had been developed.

In the past, even racing jockeys used to ride with long stirrups, with the upper part of their body erect (that is, in a full seat). The present racing seat, which takes into account the horse's balance during an extended gallop, was developed in America toward the end of the nineteenth century. At first it was ridiculed and called a "monkey seat," but the practical results it obtained soon proved its superiority over the old-fashioned way of riding races, and caused it to be generally adopted.

It is perfectly possible for the same horse, especially if it is well balanced, to perform very respectably in all of these fields of equitation when ridden by a capable rider; but, for evident reasons, its performances can hardly surpass a good average level. They cannot compare with those of horses specialized in one limited phase of the equestrian art.

On the other hand, the muscles of an animal that has been systematically and constantly trained for either collection or extension develop accordingly, so that in time they lose more or less the possibility of reacting in any other way. This is principally noticeable in horses intensively schooled in high-school dressage (shortening), and in horses that are exclusively trained for racing (extension).

The same phenomenon occurs to a certain degree in the riders. They too are transformed into specialists when they concentrate too long or too exclusively in one equestrian field or another. They then develop into dressage riders, jumping riders, huntsmen, or race riders.

A rider can choose among these different fields according to his taste and talent, after having acquired sufficient basic schooling. But, whether you practice all of these different forms of riding, simultaneously or alternately, or whether you prefer to specialize, one thing is certain: there always remains an infinite amount to learn!

3. *Continuing to Learn*

Equitation is an art in which one can never attain the highest summit, in which one never achieves absolute perfection. It never ceases to present new problems that must be solved. The more feeling, knowledge, and skill the rider possesses, the easier it is to solve them. It is, of course, personal experience that furnishes the richest instruction in this respect, but the experience of others, which can be shared by conversations with other riders or by reading good books, can also help to surmount many difficulties. The intelligent horseman lets pass no opportunity to profit from mistakes and errors, whether made by himself or observed in other riders.

His lifelong motto is "Continue to learn!"

CHAPTER 7

INSTRUCTIVE ERRORS

INSTRUCTIVE ERRORS

Errors are rather like milestones along the roads that lead to learning. And from this point of view, it is not the error itself that is so harmful, but rather its offspring, *preconception,* which in turn is the parent of *prejudice.* It is these attitudes that check our progress by preventing us from recognizing our errors and eliminating them in time.

In equitation as in life, there are many kinds of errors, big and small, foolish and intelligent, arrogant and modest. But one thing is common to them all: they are always in some way in opposition to the *laws of nature;* and this is what makes them recognizable, sooner or later.

Throughout the centuries, the equestrian world has been aroused and influenced in various ways by numerous erroneous ideas. Even today there are a number of widespread misconceptions which create more or less serious problems for the rider. Let's single out some of them here and submit them to a thorough examination.

1. *"Only a collected horse is balanced."*

In medieval times, the equestrian art in Europe was entirely under the influence of chivalry. The heavy armor worn by the knights and their steeds necessitated a heavily built horse that was as skilled and as controlled as possible at slow gaits and maneuvers in place. Speed was only of secondary importance, as well as being too much to demand of such a massive and heavily burdened horse. Nor was much expected in this respect from the rider, who, far from agile in his heavy armor, sat in the saddle or, rather, stood in the stirrups, with outstretched legs (long stirrup leathers). This tradition, passed down through the centuries, resulted in a highly specialized equestrian style which reached its climax in the *haute école* (high-school dressage).

Although the age of chivalry and the conditions it created outlived their usefulness much earlier, its equestrian methods, exclusively based on the technique developed in those olden days, actually survived until the first decades of the present century. Riders continued to sit upright, with long stirrup leathers, in their *deep saddles* (in the U.S. cavalry, it was the McClellan, or trooper's, saddle), and consequently they used a *full seat,* which was considered to be the only possible and correct one. By shortening the horse, which is called collection,* the animal was balanced (its center of gravity displaced to the rear). In other words, its posture and movements were adapted to the particular kind of burden created by the rider's weight (full seat). However, in movements where an extension of the horse was necessary (a displacement of its center of gravity toward the front), as occurs principally during the gallop and in jumping, the horse's balance was quite upset by this kind of seat, whose only advantage was to assure the rider's own balance. The rider naturally felt the resulting stiffness and insecurity of the horse's movements; but while he recognized the effect, he was unable to analyze its mechanical causes, and so he drew the incorrect deduction that *"only a collected horse is balanced."*

Not until the second half of the nineteenth century was there introduced in England a flat saddle, the so-called *English saddle,*

---

* Collection is, in fact, an actual mechanical shortening of the horse and not an illusion, as is most often taught.

on which the somewhat shorter stirrup leathers are fixed farther forward. Thus the rider assumed more of a sitting position, which permitted him to remain out of the saddle during every second beat of the trot, that is, to rise to the trot. Since the *rising* or *posting trot* (which is also called on the European continent the "English trot") was less tiring for the rider as well as for the horse than was the old seat, this method of trotting also spread to Continental Europe (although it was not immediately understood or accepted by the equestrian authorities there, and for a long time was used only for hacking) (Fig. 43).

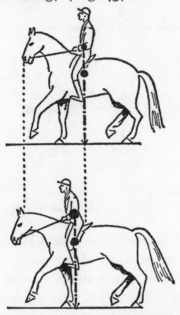

FIG. 43. *The sitting trot and the rising trot.*

Some years later, toward the end of the nineteenth century, there appeared in America the *racing saddle*, which, because of its forward-sloping flaps and its very short stirrup leathers, fixed even farther to the front of the saddle, made possible the *racing seat*. This seat was generally adopted by the American riders because of the obviously superior results it obtained in racing, and for the same reason it was soon imitated by the European jockeys as well. But since its mechanics were not really understood (there was vague talk of "unburdening" the hindquarters), and since it was considered unattractive, the "monkey seat," as it was disdain-fully called, was not accorded very much importance except at the race track* (Fig. 44).

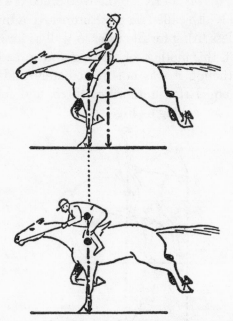

FIG. 44. *The old and the modern racing seats.*

At the turn of the century, the Italian Captain Caprilli taught a new *jumping seat,* from which developed the *hunting seat.* In order to accommodate this seat, which was not unlike the Ameri-can racing seat, the *Italian saddle* was created, with flaps some-what less forward than on the racing saddle and with stirrup leathers somewhat longer. Even Caprilli, that excellent rider who perished prematurely and tragically in a jumping accident and thus left practically no written notes, seems to have been im-pressed by the new racing seat and to have sensed what was right in a practical way, without having fathomed the underlying me-chanical reasons for its effectiveness. The jumping seat was dem-onstrated by the Italian riders for the first time in 1901 at the

* Beauty is a subjective and therefore variable notion which has frequently misled students of the art of riding. The fact is that in equitation what is "beautiful" is not necessarily correct, but what is correct is invariably beautiful.

International Horse Show in Turin, and later in 1908 at London, with such striking success that it became the common property of the equestrian world after the First World War (Fig. 45).

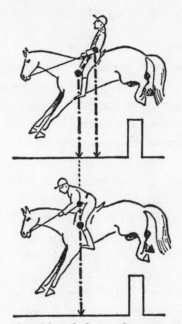

FIG. 45. *The old and the modern jumping seats.*

Due to these four phases of evolution, today we have at our disposal four different kinds of riding seats: the *full seat* (normal or school seat); the *forward-inclined seat* (the rising trot also belongs here); the *half seat* (jumping seat, hunting seat); and the *racing seat* (Fig. 11). Thus the seat has become the instrument for producing an *extensive range of actions*, while controlling and utilizing the *entire* scale of the horse's balance. But only since we have learned in recent years to understand the mechanical principles of the equestrian art* has it become possible to recognize the effects and the intrinsic qualities of these four seats: *Not only is the rider able to adapt the horse's balance to his erect seat by collection; he can also adapt his seat to the balance of a horse that is extended.*

* They were explained for the first time in my book *Reiter und Pferd im Gleichgewicht*, Albert Müller Verlag A.-G., Ruschlikon Zurich, 1940.

2. "A balanced horse places an equal burden on each of its four legs."

Riding literature abounds in various theories concerning equilibrium which employ such terms as "center of gravity," "burdening," "unburdening," "concord," and "harmony." But all of these theories are, in one way or another, in conflict with the laws of mechanics, and therefore are unable to provide us with a correct and clear conception of the elements which are responsible for the horse's balance during all its movements.* It is often said that the horse's center of gravity acts like a leaden ball in a closed tube, rolling back or forth at every movement of the tube. According to Ludwig Koch (*Die Reitkunst im Bilde*), the horse possesses not one but *two* centers of gravity, one in the forehand and the other in the hindquarters. W. Seunig (*Horsemanship*) talks very mysteriously about a "dynamic equilibrium" which, during motion, must replace the "static" one. And W. Museler (*Riding Logic*), who deals in detail with the equilibrium problems of horse and rider, believes that the rider using the jumping, hunting, and racing seats shifts his center of gravity *in front of* that of the horse in order to adapt himself to the *speed* of the movement. Several other equestrian authors share this opinion. Museler substantiates his theory by citing the example of the juggler who, in order to balance an upright pole on his outstretched palm when running, inclines the pole more or less forward. Museler's error lies primarily in the assumption that the horse's center of gravity always remains *constant* under the rider, who is sitting upright in the saddle; and he also makes the mistake of applying the laws that govern the rider's *own* balance (by inclining the juggler's pole forward, the inertia of its mass is counteracted and its balance is thereby adapted to the movement) to the *common* equilibrium, that is, the equilibrium of the horse burdened by the

---

* Mechanics = the science of acting forces; it is subdivided into dynamics, which is the science of movement through acting forces; and statics, which is the science of the equilibrium of acting forces.

rider, which is the only kind of equilibrium concerned in this particular instance. This is the basic source of all of Museler's other misconceptions concerning the problem of equilibrium, and particularly of his evident embarrassment when attempting to explain the importance of the forward seat upon landing after a jump and when riding up- or downhill (when the horse usually develops very little speed).*

One of these faulty theories is the erroneous principle which is widely taught today that *a balanced horse places an equal burden on each of its four legs.*

As with all organisms, including human beings, whose movements are produced by means of muscular power, the forward movement of the horse depends on the alternate loss and reestablishment of balance, that is to say, on dynamic and static laws. With the aid of the *propulsive power* of its legs, the horse *upsets* the equilibrium of the existing forces (the force of gravity and the force of support) and consequently upsets *the equilibrium of its center of gravity.* In this way the animal's body is set into motion, the course of which (form of movement) is determined by the product of the propulsive power and the force of gravity (position of the center of gravity). In order to avoid falling, the horse intercepts the movement of its mass at the decisive moment with supporting strength of its legs, that is to say, he *equilibrates* the acting forces (the forces of gravity and propulsion) and thus its *center of gravity* as well. The horse immediately upsets this restored balance again, and so maintains a continuous forward movement.

The position of the center of gravity (posture) governs the distribution of the force of gravity on the horse's legs and thereby determines the kind of movement that will be produced. Thus it is obvious that a race horse places a greater burden on the forelegs (by displacing its center of gravity toward the front), and a dressage horse on the hindquarters (by displacing the center of

* This is not to say that Museler's *Riding Logic* is wrong in its teachings, but only that even excellent riding instructors do not always know *why* what they teach is right.

gravity toward the rear) to a degree dependent on the particular kind of movement. And nevertheless—in fact, for this very reason —both horses are in balance.* Even where the lateral pairs of legs are concerned, it is undeniable that during certain movements (by a lateral displacement of the center of gravity) they carry unequal burdens. Consequently, *in certain circumstances the horse even burdens each one of its four legs differently; in fact, it is in just this way that it is able to maintain its balance.*

When the horse is carrying a rider, there is the additional *force of gravity of the rider's weight* which does not interfere with the acting forces, that is to say, which can be equilibrated by them only when it acts *on the same weight vector* as the horse's force of gravity. To obtain this, the rider, either by means of collection (shortened movements) or by using an appropriate seat (extended movements), must co-ordinate his center of gravity with that of the horse and thus bring into unison both of their forces of gravity. In other words, he must sit in (their common) equilibrium.** *In this way the rider distributes his weight on the horse's legs in the same natural proportion in which the horse distributes the weight of its own mass.*

3. "A certain kind of seat can 'unburden' the horse."

The racing seat and the jumping seat were developed through practical experience, by recognizing the obviously superior results they obtained during racing and jumping; both were quick to spread and both are generally accepted today. But it soon be-

* Between these two extremes of balance there exists, of course, a moment of transition during which the horse burdens its four legs equally. But this occurs only during a particular form of movement (and posture) of the horse.
** For the same reason, if you wish to sit in (common) equilibrium astride a trunk floating in the water, you must burden its center of gravity. On horseback, this is a more complicated matter because the horse changes the position of its center of gravity according to the kind of movement, and also because its balance is much more difficult to feel. However, without this equestrian sensibility—which can be and is mostly instinctive—nobody can become a real master of the art of riding.

came necessary to give these seats a theoretical explanation and a mechanical basis. Among the different theories which were devised, one in particular has prevailed until this day. It maintains that the racing seat and the jumping seat "unburden" the horse's hind legs, thereby increasing their efficiency, and that they are therefore "unburdening" or "light" seats.

If the rider sits in a full seat on a horse that has an extended posture and has therefore displaced its center of gravity toward the front (as is the case in galloping and jumping), he remains behind the horse's weight vector, thereby *overburdening* its hind legs and upsetting its balance. These are the consequences, if we take the jump as an illustrative example: First of all, the horse's take-off (propulsive power) is considerably impaired, and then, during the flight phase, its hindquarters assume a sloping position to the rear, like a javelin whose shaft is too heavy; the inevitable result is a fault made by the hind legs.

The horse's balance is also upset if the rider leans too far forward, so that he sits in front of the horse's weight vector (which, of course, will happen only in certain circumstances). The result is that the rider *overburdens* the horse's front legs, preventing the forehand from achieving the necessary elevation during the take-off; furthermore, during the flight phase, the animal's body assumes a forward inclination which results in too steep a landing, like a javelin whose point is too heavy.

A seat which leans sideways also upsets the balance of a horse that is in a straight position, because the rider deviates laterally from the horse's weight vector and thereby *overburdens* the lateral pair of legs on the side toward which he leans. Many a horse has incurred a jumping fault only because such a one-sided seat has obliged it to seek support for its threatened lateral equilibrium by extending one of its legs prematurely.

The purpose of the jumping seat—and, in fact, of the rider's seat in general—is not at all to "unburden" the horse's hind legs, forelegs, or lateral pair of legs, since this will only handicap the other pair of legs, but to *avoid overburdening* any one of the horse's legs. And this purpose can be achieved only if the rider maintains his center of gravity above that of the horse (that is, only if both weight vectors are on the same line).* In this way the rider's weight is distributed on the horse's legs in the same ratio as the horse's own mass; it does not interfere with the animal's balance, and therefore does not impede its efficiency.** This kind of seat, which requires of the rider a delicate feeling for the horse's ever-changing state of balance, is therefore not at all a seat for "un-burdening" the horse, but a *seat in equilibrium.*

4.   "When jumping or riding downhill, the rider should always use the half seat."

The kind of seat used by the rider should be determined by the horse's balance. This principle has already been recognized, but the same cannot be said for a clear conception of the mechanical effects of the rider's seat on the horse's balance. Not so very long ago, in fact, in accordance with the old academic riders' theories of equilibrium, riders were supposed to sit *absolutely erect* in the saddle during all the horse's movements (in order to burden the horse's four legs "equally"); and so they also had to lean the upper part of the body as far backward as the perpendicular when landing after a jump or when riding downhill. Now, everyone recognizes that *this was an error.* Today, thanks to Caprilli and his new school, the prevailing rule is that the rider *must always lean forward* (in order to "unburden" the horse's hind legs). However, this theory is also derived from a misunderstanding of the laws of equilibrium, and it too is *erroneous in its present form.* The truth is that both methods, old and new, are partially correct; that is, each one is valid, but in different circumstances. Only by reducing

* Only in exceptional cases when the rider wishes to check an undesirable move-ment of the horse should he deliberately upset the equilibrium necessary for the movement and thus interrupt the movement itself. For example, he may have to prevent a horse from rearing or from kicking by overburdening the forehand in the first case, or by overburdening the hindquarters in the second.
** As an example of the same principle, neither the equilibrium nor the flight of a javelin is disturbed if a metal ring is placed around the shaft at its center of gravity, though both would be if the ring were fastened in front of or behind the center of gravity.

their correct elements to a common denominator can we arrive at a universally applicable rule.

The factors of equilibrium which determine the rider's seat when landing after a jump and when riding downhill depend not only on the horse's posture (displacement of the center of gravity), as happens on the flat; they also depend (and especially so) on the horse's position in relation to the horizontal line, and therefore on the accompanying *transference of its center of gravity*. Consequently, when the steepness of the landing after a jump or

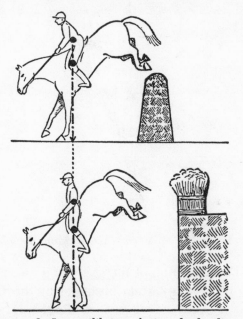

FIG. 46. *In equilibrium during the landing.*

of downhill riding is moderate, the rider should take an appropriate *forward seat*. But the more nearly the angle of the horse's back and the horizontal line approaches a right angle, the less the rider should lean forward, until finally, when the steepness of the landing or slope exceeds a certain point, the rider can co-ordinate his center of gravity with that of the horse (sit in equilibrium) *only by sitting absolutely vertically in relation to the ground* (Figs. 46 and 47).

FIG. 47. *In equilibrium when riding downhill.*

A practical confirmation of the governing mechanical laws can be found by observing certain obstacles of the Grand National Steeplechase at Aintree (Liverpool, England). Their massive dimensions (requiring a steep angle of ascent on the take-off) and in particular the sharp drops on the landing side (such as the famous Becher's Brook) generally cause such a steep landing that the slightest overburdening of the forehand by the rider (leaning forward in front of the horse's weight vector) results in loss of equilibrium and a fall.* The English jockeys are well aware of this, and while they may not understand the reasons why, they

---

* According to the same laws, the greater the angle of ascent, the lower the landing area and the farther forward the center of gravity, the more sharply will a thrown javelin come down to earth.

nevertheless lean their body more or less *backward* when landing.* This is often violently criticized by their Continental col-
leagues, some of whom, on the strength of a somewhat naïve
oversimplification of these mechanical problems, believe that the
more difficult the jump (or downhill plane) the more "unburdening" should be the rider's seat (jumping seat, hunting seat). But
the English jockeys do not enter into theoretical discussions and
unwaveringly stick to their kind of seat, for they know only too
well from years of experience that with such obstacles *this is
often the only kind of seat that is able to avoid a fall.*

But there is no need to have ridden in the Grand National in
order to have had similar experiences. When jumping obstacles
and riding across country, for example, one can encounter on a
smaller scale obstacles or slopes whose nature and condition
oblige the horse to make an unusually steep landing or descent.
(Quite often it is a mistake of horse or rider that is responsible
for the steepness of the landing.) In such cases, every sensitive
rider, perhaps only instinctively and unconsciously, will *lean his
body less forward in order to preserve the horse's balance.***

5.   *"Centrifugal force is responsible for the placement of the horse's center of gravity during all movements on a circle."*

As we have seen, it is erroneous—but unfortunately still common-
place—to teach riding students that the forward seat (hunting,

---

* Even though they may sometimes exaggerate, in this particular situation the
overburdening of the hindquarters (leaning behind the horse's weight vector) is
by far the lesser error, which can even serve in some circumstances as a counter-
weight that helps to maintain the equilibrium.
** When riding downhill, where the stability of the forelegs is greater than
when landing after a jump, these disturbances of balance are less apparent. In fact,
when riding downhill, a fall is less apt to be provoked by the overburdening of the
forelegs (leaning forward in front of the horse's weight vector) than by the overburdening of the strongly flexed and consequently less supporting hind legs. Moreover, both of these riding faults are partially corrected by the horse itself as it
raises its neck and head in the first case (displacing the center of gravity backward), and lowers them in the second place (displacing the center of gravity to
the front), thus creating a counterbalance by means of its own mass.

jumping, racing seats) is motivated by the speed of the movement and not by the extension of the horse. While it is perfectly true that during fast movements the rider can counteract the inertia of his weight by using the half seat and thus maintain his *own* balance, it is nevertheless the horse's *extension* which displaces the animal's center of gravity forward and obliges the rider to take a more forward-inclined seat in order to maintain the *common* equilibrium. The great misunderstanding of this truth probably stems from the fact that speed is always related to extension, but that extension does not always imply speed.

A similar instance of confounding cause with effect is the error made by Hans von Heydebreck and other authors influenced by him* when they claim that *the position of the center of gravity in a horse that moves on a circle, and consequently the weight ratio of its lateral pairs of legs, is not the result of the animal's lateral flexion but of centrifugal force.*

When the horse's body is *bent laterally,* its center of gravity is *displaced* toward the inside (in relation to its mass and therefore to the supporting surface as well). The horse is able to maintain its balance by increasing the weight load on the inside pair of legs, and especially on the inside hind leg, which is more flexed than the outside one and which, in order to support the animal's weight, takes a position underneath the displaced center of gravity. This effect of lateral flexion is invariable, whether the horse is standing still or moving on a straight line or a curved one.

Centrifugal force, on the other hand, is created only during movements on a circular line, and its intensity depends on the speed of the movement; it is negligible at the walk and hardly more significant at the collected trot; but it increases with speed to become quite noticeable at the canter and especially the gallop. In order to avoid losing its balance, the horse leans its body more or less obliquely toward the center of the circular line; in doing so, its center of gravity is not displaced but is *transferred* inward

* For instance, W. Seunig, who had read the manuscript of my book, *Reiter und Pferd im Gleichgewicht,* and who four years later in his book *Von der Koppel bis zur Kapriole* adapted my theories of equilibrium, without, however, always understanding and applying them correctly.

(in relation only to the supporting surface, and not to its mass), so that the inside pair of legs becomes more burdened. However, the support that is thus created for the transferred center of gravity (whose weight vector may fall outside of the supporting surface) is very insecure, and consequently the horse's adjusted balance is precarious too.

Lateral flexion and centrifugal force are therefore two independent factors whose causes and effects are *different*. They may be present one at a time or both together, and for this reason it is not always easy to separate distinctly their respective effects on the equilibrium of the horse and rider.

As a general rule, when riding on a circle, the rider should always bend his horse to the inside and give his seat an adequate inward inclination. The resulting displacement of the horse's center of gravity and the inclination of the rider's seat are both *centripetal,* with the result that the rider not only brings his seat in harmony with the horse's balance, but is also able to counteract the centrifugal force created by the circular movement. And this is the only possible way for the rider, when riding on a circle, a turn, or a curve, to be able *to sit, not only in (common) equilibrium with the horse, but also to maintain his own balance.*

An exception to this rule is the *countercanter,* because the effects of lateral flexion and centrifugal force are more or less in mutual opposition during this gait. In order to preserve the horse's correct canter position (outward flexion), the rider must sit in equilibrium, and so he must incline his seat sufficiently *outward* while safeguarding his own balance (which has been made insecure by the centrifugal force) with the aid of his muscles. However, since the countercanter is generally performed at a shortened rhythm which reduces the effect of the centrifugal force, and only for brief periods of time, the rider should have little trouble in overcoming this difficulty.

Not subject to this rule are unmounted horses moving at liberty (who are able to assume a much more insecure balance) and mounted horses that have been insufficiently trained (straightened). These horses lean more or less to the outside when going around a curve, without bending their bodies at all or even, as is often the case, bending them to the wrong side (outward). In such a situation, the rider must not incline his body inward, for this would *not* bring his center of gravity into unison with that of the horse and would, in fact, only imperil the horse's already unstable balance. On the contrary, he should instinctively sit more or less *upright,* or lean somewhat to the *outside,* even if this requires him to maintain his own balance (which is being disturbed by the effects of centrifugal force) exclusively by means of muscular effort.

Lateral flexion is one of the most important factors affecting equilibrium, both during schooling (straightening the horse) and when riding in general. It is lateral flexion and not centrifugal force that *decides,* in principle, *the position of the center of gravity on the horse's transverse axis, the weight ratio of its legs, as well as the mechanics of its movements, and thus determines exactly how the rider should sit in equilibrium.*

6.   *"The trot is a stepping gait."*

Errors can slip into the writings of even the best-known authorities, for, as we all know, anybody can make mistakes. But because of the prestige of the writers, certain misconceptions have been generally accepted and indiscriminately repeated. To this category belongs the erroneous but widespread belief that *the trot is not a springing but a stepping gait.*

In the normal correct trot, there occurs after each of its beats a phase in the air which is easily demonstrable. But how can a horse step and yet become air-borne? How can it fly without jumping or springing? To be sure, the more collected the trot, the briefer is this phase of suspension, so that in actual practice it may finally disappear entirely. But a similar phase also occurs during the canter, and yet nobody contests that the canter is a springing gait.

The *trot is a springing gait* in which the horse springs alternately with the diagonal pairs of legs. Consequently, the trot (two beats) differs basically from *the walk,* which is a true *striding* gait, in which each lateral pair of feet is placed separately on the ground (four beats) so that the horse always maintains some direct contact with the surface.*

Of all the gaits, the trot has the *least pendulum movement,* and since the horse must compensate for this by increasing its muscular effort, it uses the trot only rarely when at liberty. This is also the reason why the horse can be ridden in a shortened posture (collection) at an extended trot, a thing that is impossible at an extended canter (gallop) or an extended walk, both of which require long pendulum movements and therefore a more extended posture.

The *canter* is also a springing gait. But it differs from the trot, not only in its particular sequence of hoofbeats (three beats), but also in the resulting oscillation of the forehand and hindquarters, for which the horse's center of gravity serves as an axis, and which is much more pronounced in the canter than in the trot.

The *rein-back* (backing) is a striding gait in which the feet of each diagonal pair of legs are put down separately (four beats). The horse initiates the movement with one of the front legs, stepping backward immediately afterward with the diagonal hind leg. It is therefore an error to say that the rein-back is a form of trot, although this statement is sometimes made.

All these differences in the sequence of hoofbeats are caused by mechanical factors and they are of great importance to the rider. He must know, feel, and understand them if he is to influence his horse correctly and effectively.

For example, when striking off into a canter from a walk, the rider must co-ordinate his aids with the walking beat during which the horse places the *outside hind leg* (in terms of the proposed canter) on the ground and thus places it farther forward underneath its body than the inside one. The horse can now easily shift its entire weight onto the outside hind leg and easily go

---

* While Henry Wynmalen, who is an authority in England, writes in his book *Equitation* that the collected walk has a diagonal hoof sequence of two beats, we can be sure that his idea of a "collected walk" is not a walk at all but a slow trot without impulsion.

into the hoofbeat pattern of the canter, taking this beat of the walk as the first beat of the canter.

In the trot, the aids for the canter must be co-ordinated with the trotting beat during which the *outside hind leg* and the *inside foreleg* are put down, so that the first beat of the canter is made by the outside hind leg. This transition from one hoofbeat sequence to the other is more difficult for both horse and rider due to mechanical reasons, and that is why the first lessons in striking off into a canter should always start from a walk.

If the rider immediately strikes off into a canter from a rein-back (without making a momentary halt in between), he must apply the necessary aids at the moment in which the horse raises its *inside foreleg*, because then the outside hind leg, placed underneath the horse's body, will be induced to assume the burden and to start the canter immediately, thus making the raised inside foreleg the "leading leg." If the preceding rein-back consists of an even number of steps, it is best to have the horse start this backing movement with the inside foreleg (inside rein); on the other hand, when the rein-back consists of an uneven number of steps, it should be initiated by the outside foreleg (outside rein).

7. *"The principal purpose of the rising trot (posting trot) is to promote the rider's comfort."*

How often do we see riders (usually dressage riders) who rise to the trot from "elastic" ankle joints, with the upper part of the body completely upright. They are of the opinion, more or less openly avowed, that the posting trot plays only a very secondary role in the art of riding. They regard it only as a simple means of *promoting the rider's comfort.*

It is amazing how many prejudices and false conceptions are still rampant today concerning the rising trot. They hark back to the early days when the riders' only interest in the posting trot and its manner of execution was to increase their own comfort, and, as a matter of fact, it was because of the comfortable relief it affords that the posting trot found favor and was adopted by the equestrian world.

In those days, the only equestrian art that was known was school riding (dressage). Its aim was (and still is today) to school the horse in collected movements and thus to develop primarily the *bearing power* of the hindquarters, which can be achieved only if the rider uses a full seat, and collects the horse by engaging its hind legs well underneath its body. Therefore, the trot in all its forms, from the piaffer to the extended trot, was always ridden in a shortened posture and in a full seat (Fig. 48). In this kind of

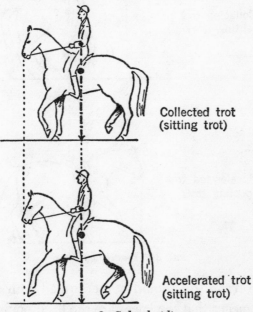

Collected trot
(sitting trot)

Accelerated trot
(sitting trot)

FIG. 48. *School riding.*

method there was, of course, no place for the posting trot, which at best—when adjusted to the shortened posture of the horse, with the rider's body erect—was tolerated only occasionally as a reposing diversion for the rider.

However, with the increasing development of practical riding, whose varied activities require primarily *propulsive power* from the hindquarters, the rising trot developed into a balanced seat.

This enables the rider to sit in equilibrium during the faster trotting paces, which create a more extended posture of the horse and displace its center of gravity toward the front.* When posting to the trot, the rider should follow the horse's movement by inclining the upper part of his body suitably forward (as in the half seat for a medium canter), which is possible only if his knees and legs, always ready to act, are sufficiently secure (Fig. 49). Conse-

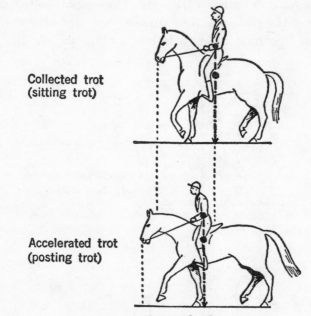

Collected trot
(sitting trot)

Accelerated trot
(posting trot)

FIG. 49. *Practical riding.*

quently, the rising trot should be performed with a *strong knee grip*, which means that the knees are the fixed point of the rider's seat (and not with elastic ankle joints, which inevitably give the legs and knees a gliding, up-and-down movement).

The rising trot is therefore a balanced seat, which places at the rider's disposition a vast and finely graduated range of weight actions *with the aim of improving the horse's performance, and not the rider's comfort.*

* Just as the rider's weight distribution depends upon his seat, so does the quality of the horse's performance depend upon his weight distribution.

8. *"The rider should always post on the outside diagonal."*

As long as the posting trot was practiced only on roads and trails, in other words, on more or less straight lines, the question of which diagonal to post on at the trot was of no importance, so long as the diagonal was changed at regular intervals. But as the rising trot became more and more widespread and finally was used extensively in the riding school (dressage ring), where riding on circles and therefore flexing the horse is one of the most important exercises, the question had to be faced and settled, if only for reasons of uniformity. And so most of the military riding instructions in the majority of the European countries decreed that *the rider should always post on the outside (fore)leg.**

A horse bent on a circle flexes its inside hind leg more than the outside one and places it farther forward underneath its body, that is to say, more or less underneath its center of gravity, which has been displaced toward the inside because of the horse's bending. This causes the inside hind leg, whose supporting power has already been decreased because of its stretched position, to be considerably more burdened than the other legs; furthermore, it not only has to bear more weight than the other hind leg, but also has to push off more than the other hind leg. When posting on the outside leg, that is, when sitting down in the saddle as the outside foreleg strikes the ground, the rider burdens it of course, but he also burdens the inside (diagonal) hind leg at the same time, and to a much greater degree. In fact, he overburdens the inside hind leg. The horse's only defense in this situation is to place this inside hind leg less far underneath its body (sometimes it also places the hind leg sideways) and to flex its body less strongly; and, needless to say, this behavior is just the opposite of what we are trying

---

* Due to an old tradition that ignores the much more important role played by the hind legs, we speak of a posting trot on the outside or on the inside leg, always meaning the *fore*leg in question.

to obtain by working on a circle, namely, *to school the horse in engaging its hind legs well underneath its body and in producing lateral flexion.*

The truth of the above statement can easily be proven by practical experience. A horse that is usually ridden at a posting trot on the outside foreleg can also be ridden without the slightest difficulty on the inside one, because this unburdens the inside hind leg. The rider can make excellent use of this by urging the horse, through forward driving, to place its inside leg farther underneath its body and to increase its flexion. On the other hand, a horse that has always been ridden at the rising trot on the *inside* foreleg will resist such a change of leg more or less strenuously. It perceptibly *shortens* the stride of its hind leg, which is now overburdened by the change, its gait becomes less elastic, and its bending noticeably *decreases.* The horse opposes this increased burdening of its inside hind leg because it impairs its balance.

From the point of view of the rider's aids as well, there are valid reasons for discouraging the practice of posting on the outside foreleg. The rider can *drive with his legs* much better when sitting in the saddle than when out of it, and when the hind leg that is to be driven farther under the body is moving and not placed on the ground. In order to drive effectively the inside hind leg (which in this case is the principal one to be urged forward) the rider must *be sitting in the saddle* at the exact moment when this leg reaches forward in unison with the *outside* foreleg, which is to say that the rider must *rise* to the trot on the *inside* foreleg. Furthermore, this way of trotting permits a much more delicate and varied use of the *inside rein.* Since this rein must co-operate with the rider's leg when flexing the horse, it can profitably become more *active* when the inside hind leg is on the ground (and consequently is not being driven by the rider's leg). However, if the same active rein aid were applied as this leg steps forward, the result would be to impede it from placing itself underneath the horse's body.

The riding instructions compiled by the cavalry were considered equestrian law, not only for the army riders, but also for all equestrian competitions in the country concerned, including the participating civilian riders. They were so widely accepted that nobody dreamed of questioning their infallibility. Today, however, since the mounted cavalry has ceased to exist almost everywhere, the military riding instructions have begun to lose much of their former authority. And so it is to be hoped that in the near future, the young, unprejudiced generation of riders will recognize that *the recommendation of the posting trot on the outside foreleg is an error, and at last discard it.*

9. *"The rider's forearms should be held horizontally."*

After the Olympic Games in London in 1948, there was much discussion in the international equestrian press concerning the Individual Dressage Test. There was criticism of the judges as well as of the riders, and especially of the Gold Medal winner, whom many observers reproached for holding his hands too high. To answer this accusation, a compatriot who had been a judge of the Three Day Event Dressage Test during the same games and who was considered an eminent riding expert in his country, wrote in a brusque and authoritative article the following opinion, which was undoubtedly shared by other horsemen throughout the world: "His forearms were absolutely horizontal and therefore the position of his hands was perfectly correct."

In order to fulfill their functions effectively, the reins must act through the bit on the exceedingly sensitive, toothless edge of the lower jaw that is called the bars, and this is possible only if the horse possesses suitable neck and head carriage. The range of every horse's neck and head carriage is established by its individual conformation; within these natural limits, its particular placement is determined by the kind of movement that is being performed. A correct head and neck carriage is the preliminary essential condition for establishing a permanent, elastic contact between the rider's hands and the horse's mouth, without which effective rein actions are impossible.

In some cases, the horse tries to shift the action of the bit from the bars to the elastic and less sensitive corners of the mouth by lowering or raising its head and neck (thus getting "in front of" or "over" the bit), or else tries to evade it entirely by drawing back the mouth (getting "behind" the bit). The form of resistance a particular horse selects is by no means a matter of chance; on the contrary, it depends primarily on the animal's conformation, that is to say, on its individual elements of equilibrium, and it can therefore easily be anticipated by an experienced rider. However, it is a great mistake to suppose that the rider can correct too low a neck and head carriage by raising his hands, and too high a carrige by lowering them. In fact, both of these actions produce the contrary effect. Instead of helping to make the correct head and neck carriage easier and more comfortable for the horse by a sensible use of the reins (with the assistance of the leg aids), they make it more difficult and sometimes impossible for the horse to hold its head and neck correctly. Furthermore, the horse is obliged to remain in a more or less perceptible state of opposition until it finally accepts the unpleasant situation and becomes accustomed to it. The final result is a "spoiled" horse, whose principal fault is invariably that it is insufficiently or not at all *on the bit*.

A horse that is *well on the bit* (in hand) not only accepts the action of the bit on the bars of the mouth, but seeks the *contact with the reins* that the rider should permanently maintain by means of his *sensitive feeling* (Fig. 50).

FIG. 50. *The horse is on the bit.*

In order to place a horse well on the bit (in hand), in fact, in order to apply the rein aids correctly during all of the horse's movements, which often involve considerable changes of posture, the rider's hands must become a sensitive instrument of transmitting power that reacts quickly and distinctly to the slightest change; and this is only possible if they act *between the elbows and the horse's mouth in an absolutely straight, unbroken line* (Figs. 51 and 52). Only the straightest, shortest line of communi-

Wrong

Right

FIG. 51. *Rein action when the head carriage is too low.*
FIG. 52. *Rein action when the head carriage is too high.*

cation leading from the muscles of the upper arm, passing through free elbow and wrist-joints to reach the horse's mouth (or inversely), with the arms supple* and independent of the rider's seat, can produce the *sensitivity and lightness of hand* that are

---

* If the arms are supple and independent of the rider's seat, the hands will be supple and independent too; on the other hand, the reverse of this statement is not necessarily true.

necessary in order to act effectively with the reins in every situation (Fig. 53).

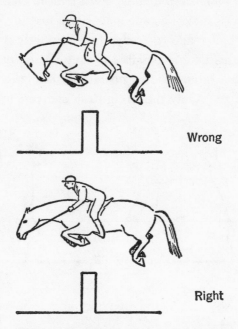

Wrong

Right

FIG. 53. *Rein action during the jump.*

The inevitable conclusion to be drawn from this is that under ordinary circumstances, with a normally schooled horse that is well in hand and accepts the bit, *the rider's forearms must not take a horizontal position; they should form a more or less obtuse angle with the upper arm, depending on the kind of movement (posture) of the horse* (Fig. 50).

Of all the aids, correct rein actions are the most difficult to master, partly because the flexibility of our hands and arms permits infinitely varied manipulations of the reins, and partly because the remarkable flexibility of the horse's neck and head enables it to oppose these delicate rein actions very easily and successfully. And this is often the reason why sometimes even good horsemen do not always use their hands correctly.

10. "The haute école (high-school dressage) is the highest form of equestrian art."

Certain erroneous equestrian beliefs, because of their glorious past, still exercise a fascinating power of attraction for many horsemen. Such an error is the opinion of so many riders that *the high school is the* summum *and the absolutely highest achievement of the entire equestrian art.*

High-school dressage, whose aim is confined to collected movements, often performed in place, and which therefore strives to obtain the horse's maximum degree of collection, is only one specialized field in the realm of equitation. In regard to the kinds of movements performed and the means and methods of producing them, it represents one extreme of the equestrian art, the opposite extreme being represented by racing, which is exclusively concerned with extended movements and thus with the utmost possible extension of the horse (Fig. 54). Consequently, both of these activities hold an exceptional position in equitation; both require of the rider as well as of the horse an appropriately specialized training which finally results, as is the case of all specializations, in a certain one-sidedness.*

During the course of an evolution that lasted some hundred years (and that was founded in the beginning on the *erroneous belief* that only a collected horse is in equilibrium), high-school dressage has undoubtedly reached the zenith of perfection in its field. Until the first decade of this century, even though it had long since lost its practical value, the *haute école* was universally accepted as the exclusive example of true equestrian art, and even now is incontestably "the classical equestrian art," the pillar of our glorious traditions and of our equestrian culture. Although riding across country and over obstacles became ever more im-

---

* All the other fields of the equestrian art that lie between the two extremes of high-school dressage and racing, and whose activities serve various practical purposes, are called practical riding.

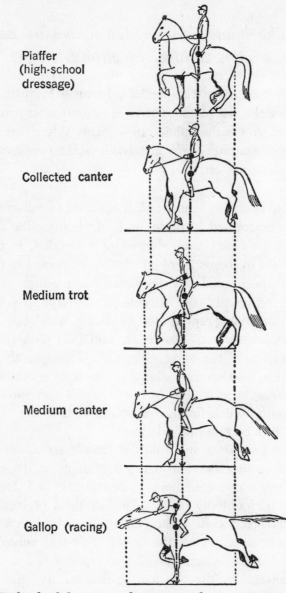

Piaffer
(high-school
dressage)

Collected canter

Medium trot

Medium canter

Gallop (racing)

FIG. 54. *High-school dressage and racing are the two extremes of the equestrian art.*

portant, there were no means in those days which enabled the rider to accommodate himself to the horse's balance during extended movements and thus to exploit fully its capabilities. However, in recent decades, now that riders everywhere have learned to know and use the different kinds of balanced seats, the achievements in the other equestrian activities that previously had lagged behind have made such tremendous strides that today, though they may be of a different nature, *in regard to performance, they are absolutely the equal of the* haute école.

11. *"This horse is not sufficiently collected."*

Occasionally one hears it said even by riding instructors, dressage judges, and other experts: "Although this horse has performed the test correctly, it is not sufficiently collected."

This statement is nothing else but a contradiction in terms, and reveals the presence of a fundamental error. The fact is that collection is not an end in itself, but only the means to an end. And the end or goal in this case is the test in question. If the horse has performed it correctly, then it must have been sufficiently collected; if the collection was insufficient, the execution of the movement could not possibly have been faultless. Only the end, the performance, should determine the equestrian means and methods used to achieve it; therefore, there exists no visual model, no ideal pattern of the horse's posture—that is, of its degree of collection: *The horse's posture and collection are exclusively determined by the animal's conformation and by the kind of movement being performed.*

The shorter the movement, the more bearing power must be supplied by the horse's hindquarters (engaging the hind legs underneath the body), and this is obtained only at the expense of its propulsive power, which thus becomes the measure of its degree of collection. *The rider must never collect his horse more than is necessary for the (correct) performance of the movement in question.*

We have reviewed and examined above certain riding problems and tried to bring them into harmony with the laws of nature. My aim has been, not only to substitute clear conceptions and correct principles for misunderstandings and erroneous beliefs, but also to demonstrate that the equestrian evolution which has been taking place since primeval times is still very much alive today, and that it requires the collaboration of all riders.

Thus it is especially important for young, serious, and unprejudiced riders to study and ponder these and similar problems, in order to arrive eventually at solutions for themselves based on their own experience and judgment. *For it is the young riders who are and must be responsible for continuing the eternal progress of the equestrian art.*